*Women's Colleges and Universities
in a Global Context*

Women's Colleges and Universities in a Global Context

KRISTEN A. RENN

Johns Hopkins University Press

Baltimore

© 2014 Johns Hopkins University Press
All rights reserved. Published 2014
Printed in the United States of America on acid-free paper
2   4   6   8   9   7   5   3   1

Johns Hopkins University Press
2715 North Charles Street
Baltimore, Maryland 21218-4363
www.press.jhu.edu

Library of Congress Cataloging-in-Publication Data
Renn, Kristen A.
Women's colleges and universities in a global context / Kristen A. Renn.
pages cm.
Includes bibliographical references and index.
ISBN 978-1-4214-1477-5 (hardcover : alk. paper) — ISBN 978-1-4214-1478-2
(electronic) — ISBN 1-4214-1477-5 (hardcover : alk. paper) —
ISBN 1-4214-1478-3 (electronic) 1. Women's colleges. 2. Women's colleges—
Cross-cultural studies. 3. Women—Education. 4. Women in higher
education. I. Title.
LC1567.R46 2014
378.0082—dc23   2013050149

A catalog record for this book is available from the British Library.

Special discounts are available for bulk purchases of this book.
For more information, please contact Special Sales at
410-516-6936 or specialsales@press.jhu.edu.

Johns Hopkins University Press uses environmentally friendly
book materials, including recycled text paper that is composed of at least
30 percent post-consumer waste, whenever possible.

CONTENTS

Women's Colleges and Universities in a Global Context represents a convergence of key passions in my life and work: the study of higher education and a global perspective on girls, women, and gender equity. These commitments began during my youth as a Girl Scout and took root during my undergraduate years at Mount Holyoke College (Massachusetts, USA), one of the world's oldest continuing women's colleges. The purposeful creation of educational spaces where girls and women can be themselves, learn about one another, and strive to achieve at the highest levels inspired and inspires me. My gratitude therefore goes to the founders, supporters, and continuing stewards of these organizations and others like them that retain a commitment to freeing girls and women to imagine and reach their highest potential. I would not be who I am and this book would not be what it is without them.

I owe thanks to Mount Holyoke President Emeritus Joanne V. Creighton and former Assistant to the President Jesse Lytle, who welcomed me into the community of leaders of women's colleges and universities that makes up the organization Women's Education Worldwide (WEW). WEW brings together leaders of women's colleges and universities from dozens of nations to consider pressing issues in the education of women globally and in local contexts. Members of WEW welcomed me to their meetings and allowed me to ask questions, visit some of their campuses, and test my findings with them. Their generosity cannot be overstated.

I also thank the leaders, faculty, and students at the thirteen institutions in my study. They, too, were exceptionally generous with time, insight, hospitality, humor, logistical support, and patience. Although they number only a few hundred of the thousands of educators and students at women's colleges and universities in the world, I hope that their voices will resonate with readers and with the larger universe of institutions they are meant to represent. I have attempted to honor the experiences and voices of the women and men presented in this book, and to whatever extent I have fallen short, the responsibility is mine.

I began data collection during a sabbatical from my department at Michigan State University (MSU), and funding for a pilot for this study came from the MSU College of Education. Funding for the full international study came from the Spencer Foundation. I am grateful to both for the support and confidence in my work.

The editorial staff at Johns Hopkins University Press has been enthusiastic about this book from its inception. I appreciate the insight, patience, and good work of Jacqueline Wehmueller, Greg Britton, and freelance editor Ashleigh McKown. Each made the book better and the publishing process enjoyable.

I thank those on the home front who made it possible for me to embark on a project more ambitious than I could have accomplished without them. My colleagues in the Higher, Adult, and Lifelong Education program at MSU were superb and supportive. My students tolerated my periodic absences from campus and the occasional email lost due to inconsistent Internet access during my journeys. Family, friends, and colleagues who were recipients of my regular "travelogue" emails responded with support, sympathy, humor, and enthusiasm to my tales of research and travel discoveries, travails, missteps, gastronomic adventures, and small victories. In particular, the support of my parents Dan Renn and Carol Measom, my partner Melissa McDaniels, and my in-laws Garry and Annette McDaniels kept me motivated and confident. I am grateful to all of them.

Finally, I thank the students whom I met, saw, heard, and heard about around the world. Students at women's colleges and universities expand to fill their spaces and spill out of the confines of classrooms, cafeterias, hostels, and quads. They embrace the opportunity to inhabit, for a few years, a woman-centered learning environment that takes for granted that women can and will change the world for the better. I appreciate the privilege to be among them and to write about them.

Women's Colleges and Universities in a Global Context

CHAPTER ONE

The Context of Women's Higher Education

Educating girls and women is a route to improving societies worldwide. Health, human rights, and economic measures are more favorable in regions where girls and women have more access to education. When women have more education, literacy rates among children are higher, maternal and infant death rates are lower, HIV rates are lower, women are more politically active, and they have increased earning capacity, all of which has a positive effect on child nutrition, education levels, and health (Herz & Sperling, 2004; Roudi-Fahimi & Moghadam, 2003; UNESCO, n.d.; United Nations Development Programme, 2013). The United Nations Millennium Development Goals (MDG; see United Nations, 2013) include attention to women's education and empowerment as both a measurable outcome and a strategy to achieve other outcomes (such as eradicating extreme poverty and hunger, reducing child mortality, and ensuring environmental sustainability).

As economist and Nobel laureate Amartya Sen noted, "There are few subjects that match the social significance of women's education in the contemporary world" (Sen, 2004, p. 1). Increasing levels of girls' and women's participation from basic through higher education increases their ability to get jobs, to have a voice in government and civic life, to understand and act upon their legal rights, and to make decisions within the family, including decisions related to population growth and family planning (Nussbaum, 2004; Sen, 2004). Feminist philosopher Martha Nussbaum (2004) argued, "The issue of women's education is both urgent and complex. But it has long been the neglected poor relation of the international development world, ignored by many of the most powerful thinkers and actors in this field in favor of the single goal of economic growth, which by itself delivers little to the poor of developing nations" (p. 351).

The urgency and complexity of educating women derive in part from multiple and competing policy priorities at national, state, and local levels, which are themselves located within cultural systems that influence priorities at government, community, family, and individual levels (Colclough, 2008; Robinson-Pant, 2004; Stromquist, 2012).

In this book I examine one emergent approach for addressing the urgency and complexity of educating women: women's colleges and universities. Although they represent a minority of postsecondary institutions in the world and serve a minority of all women in postsecondary education, women's colleges and universities educate hundreds of thousands of students every year. As I discuss in chapter 3, some of these women would not be able to participate in higher education if women's institutions were not available. For some students and their families, single-sex[1] education is the only acceptable option. But many students around the world choose women's colleges and universities even when they have full freedom to attend coeducational ones. This reality raises one question—*Why would someone with other options choose a women's institution?*—and leads to a larger one—*What are women's colleges and universities for in the twenty-first century?* This book is my attempt to answer these questions from the perspective of thirteen women's institutions in ten countries on five continents (Africa, Asia, Australia, Europe, and North America). The answers point to the urgency and complexity of higher education for women in local, national, and global contexts.

Women in some regions[2] (e.g., Australia, North America, Western Europe) participate in higher (also called postsecondary or tertiary) education at rates the same as or higher than do men (EdStats, 2013). But in others, including some of the most populous nations—such as India and Pakistan—women's education

1. The term *single-sex* is commonly used in reference to elementary, secondary, and postsecondary institutions that enroll students of one sex (female or male). The terms *girls, women, boys,* and *men* refer to gender, but the term *single-gender* is rarely used in research or educational practice. Historically, some institutions were founded as *female colleges,* though the term is now out of date (and grammatically troubling, as it implies that the colleges themselves had a sex). Sex and gender are related concepts, but social scientists consider them distinct. Throughout this book, I use *women's college* (or *university*) to indicate a postsecondary institution that enrolls only female students and grants degrees, including the bachelor's. *Coeducational institutions* are those that enroll women and men. *Gender-segregated institutions* enroll women and men but keep them segregated on campus (see chap. 2 for more description of gender-segregated campuses). I occasionally use *single-sex* in its colloquial meaning, which references a school that is all girls or all boys, or a college or university that is all women or all men. I am aware that this bifurcation of gender into two and only two distinct categories is itself problematic (see Butler, 1999), and caution the reader to consider the likelihood that in some of the contexts I describe there were individuals who did not conform to binary definitions of gender. Marine (2011) in one example described changing campus norms related to increased visibility of transgender students at US women's colleges.

2. *Region* can refer to a section within a country (e.g., southern China, northern Italy) or to a supranational region (e.g., the Indian subcontinent, Middle East, northern Africa,). Throughout this book, I use it to refer to the latter.

lags behind men's (EdStats, 2013). The capacity of these higher education systems does not meet demand overall, so there are large numbers of potential students left out regardless of gender, but even so, more men have access to postsecondary education than do women. In response to this reality, Joanne Creighton, former president of all-women's Mount Holyoke College (Massachusetts, United States), has called women's education "the great unfinished agenda of the 21st century" (Creighton, 2004, p. 17).

There are a number of explanations for gender inequity in higher education participation. Where women participate at higher rates than men, the reasons why include a relatively higher economic return for women than for men, girls' advantage over boys in school performance, and men's lower motivation to pursue and complete higher education (Goldin, Katz, & Kuziemko, 2006; Leppel, 2002; McDaniel, 2012; Vincent-Lancrin, 2008). Where women participate at lower rates than men, reasons include cultural, social, and religious beliefs that limit girls' and women's educational, social, and economic options (Altbach, 2004; Buchmann & Hannum, 2001; Knight 2004; Malik & Courtney, 2011; Morley, 2006b; Nussbaum, 2004; Qureshi & Rarieya, 2007; Sahni & Shankar, 2012). Globally, women remain particularly behind in participation at elite institutions and in traditional "male" fields of study including science, technology, engineering, and mathematics, or STEM (Barone, 2011; Charles & Bradley, 2009; McDaniel, 2012; Vincent-Lancrin, 2008).

Tradition, culture, religion, and economic circumstances factor into a woman's chances for education. Even if they receive an elementary school education, when girls become young adult women they may be kept home to help with household duties (e.g., farming or caring for younger children). Or they may live in areas where unmarried women (and their families) lose honor if they leave the house unaccompanied by a male relative. Families of limited means may prioritize a son's education over a daughter's, because she can act as a caretaker to younger siblings. A son will later support his parents, whereas a daughter will leave her parents' household when she marries (Jayaweera, 1997a; Malik & Courtney, 2011; Nussbaum, 2004; Radha, 2011; Sahni & Shankar, 2012). These examples illustrate a few of the ways that social class interacts with gender and culture to influence a girl's chances of persisting in education, and a discussion of gender and education cannot be undertaken out of this context (see Hyer et al., 2008; Jayaweera, 1997a, 1997b; Klasen, 2006; Morley & Lugg, 2009; Stromquist, 2012).

Around the world, women's colleges and universities represent one emergent solution to the challenge of providing access to higher education for women. In some regions (e.g., North America, East Asia, Europe) a sector of public and private women's institutions opened, expanded, and gradually closed or became coeducational as formerly all-male institutions admitted female students and competition for applicants increased (see Harwarth, 1997; Knight, 2004; Kodate, Kodate, & Kodate, 2010; Wolf-Wendel, 2002). A relative handful of these institutions, typically those that were most prestigious and well funded, have persisted as women's colleges and universities in Japan, the Philippines, South Korea, and the United States. There are also examples of women's residential colleges persisting within coeducational universities in Australia, Canada, Italy, and the United Kingdom. In other regions (Indian subcontinent, the Middle East, Southeast Asia), the sector remains robust; in nations where demand for higher education greatly outstrips capacity, there is little chance of these institutions closing or admitting men to attract more applicants. A few new women's colleges and universities—some public, some private—have opened recently in Africa, the Middle East, and South and Southeast Asia.

It is relatively easy to understand why women's institutions open and persist in regions where women are not permitted by law or custom to attend university with men. In places where single-sex or gender-segregated universities are the only feasible option for women seeking postsecondary education (as I discuss in chap. 3), they are critical in providing access. But where women have equal access to higher education, where women outnumber men in college, or where coeducation is so prevalent that few young women even consider attending a women's college, the purpose of single-sex institutions is more difficult to discern. If they are no longer, as they once were, about providing access to higher education, what are they for? What do they contribute to women's education and to society more broadly? These are the questions that motivated me to undertake an international study of women's colleges and universities. The answers point to a richness of opportunities and outcomes for students, graduates, and communities.

In the chapters that follow, I attempt to answer the question *What roles do women's colleges and universities play in a global context in the twenty-first century?* In answering it, I identified five overarching roles. First, providing access—both in absolute terms and relative to other higher education options—remains one purpose. The second role emerges from another question—*Access to what?*—and encompasses the ways in which these institutions provide educational environments that support women's success and are less hostile (i.e., free of sexual harassment and sex discrimination) than coeducational institutions. The third role relates to the specific emphasis that many women's colleges and universities place on leadership development for students and alumnae. Women at coeducational institutions may also find their way into activities that develop leadership abilities, but at many women's colleges there is an explicit focus on developing future leaders for government, business, and civil society. The fourth role women's institutions play is in gender empowerment for students, faculty, and communities. From courses to extracurricular (also called *cocurricular*) activities to community engagement, some of these colleges and universities are central agencies in empowering women in society.

The fifth role is less clearly defined but distinctive. Women's institutions play a symbolic role in society, drawing attention to the status of girls and women. They symbolize possibilities for women in education and the workforce. They also convey contradictory messages about the purposes of women's education and embody a paradox that rests on their existence as organizations that are both progressive and conservative. In some regions, these symbolic roles and contradictions raise questions about why women do not have equal access. In other regions, they raise questions about women's experiences at coeducational institutions and why some women would choose the path less traveled to an all-female student experience. As will become clear in subsequent chapters, these five themes are interrelated but distinct.

To set the stage for understanding the roles of women's colleges and universities in the twenty-first century, one must understand the current status of women's higher education worldwide, the history of women's colleges and universities, and what is known of the outcomes of attending one of them.

Current Status of Women's Higher Education Worldwide

An analysis of women's higher education necessarily begins with understanding the status of girls' elementary and secondary education. The education of girls worldwide defies simple description, though there is general agreement—especially among global funders and promoters of development such as the World Bank and Organisation for Economic Co-operation and Development (OECD)—that overall the picture is improving in the direction of gender equity (International Bank for Reconstruction and Development and the World Bank, 2011; OECD, 2013). There remain some countries, or areas within countries, where differences in girls' and boys' participation in education widen dramatically over time; in most of these cases, boys tend to stay in school longer than girls, though in parts of East Asia, Latin America, and the Pacific, girls get more education than boys (Jensen, 2011; OECD, 2013). Trends in enrollment, by gender, from primary to tertiary education are illustrated in table 1.1. "Net enrollment" refers to the percentage of individuals in the relevant age category who are enrolled in school at the three levels.

There is substantial evidence that poverty interacts with gender to exacerbate differences in educational attainment (International Bank for Reconstruction and Development and the World Bank, 2011; Jensen, 2011; OECD, 2013; UNESCO, n.d.). Poor children worldwide are less likely than their wealthier peers to stay in school, and children from minority ethnic, racial, or religious groups are less likely than majority children to get an education (UNESCO, n.d.). Combining these intersecting effects, poor girls from minority groups are the least likely of all children to get an elementary education or to achieve basic literacy (Hyer et al., 2008; Jayaweera, 1997a, 1997b; Klasen, 2006; Stromquist, 2001a, 2012; UNESCO, n.d.).

Since the 1980s, girls in some countries—both developed and developing—have achieved higher levels of education than their brothers. In the United Kingdom, more women than men complete upper secondary school (OECD, 2013). In the United States, among white and black youth, males drop out of secondary education at higher rates than females (Chapman, Laird, Ifill, & KewalRamani, 2011). Secondary enrollment in about one-third of the world—including Honduras, Namibia, Qatar, and Suriname among others—favors females over males (Fiske, 2012). One rationale for this reversal of the historic trend of more education for boys than for girls is that young men without secondary degrees may find jobs, whereas young women without secondary degrees have fewer opportunities (Charles & Grusky, 2004; Goldin et al., 2006; Vincent-Lancrin, 2008). Girls may need a secondary credential to enter the workforce in jobs deemed acceptable for their gender, but boys might not. Boys can work as agricultural and industrial laborers, drivers, housekeepers, and the like without the degree; cultural prohibitions on young women working in these and similar positions result in a higher economic reward for girls staying in school until they reach a level of education needed for finding suitable employment. McDaniel (2012) noted that a gender wage gap across industrialized nations "suggests that, for boys, more opportunities may exist than for girls, and girls may need to value schooling more and have more positive attitudes toward school than boys" (p. 43). Regardless of the reasons, basic participation metrics show a number of successes in improving access to education for girls in the past fifty years, although there is still work to be done in terms of gender equity in school attainment.

The link between children's elementary and secondary opportunities and their tertiary prospects is clear: access to basic education in childhood is a

TABLE 1.1

National comparisons of the education of boys/men and girls/women

Country	Net enrollment ratio in primary education		Girls' share of primary enrollment (%)	Net enrollment ratio in secondary education		Girls' share of secondary enrollment (%)	Gross enrollment ratio in tertiary education		Women's share of tertiary enrollment (%)	School life expectancy from primary to tertiary education (years)	
	Girls	Boys		Girls	Boys		Women	Men		Women	Men
Afghanistan	NA	NA	39	13	34	32	1	5	18	6	10
Australia	97	97	49	86	84	48	87	65	56	20	19
Canada	100	100	49	94	95	48	69	51	56	16	15
China	NA	NA	46	NA	NA	NA	25	24	49	12	11
India	89	92	47	NA	NA	NA	13	19	39	11	10
Kenya	83	82	49	49	52	47	3	5	41	11	11
Pakistan	67	81	44	29	38	42	5	6	45	6	8
Saudi Arabia	89	90	49	76	68	46	39	35	52	14	15
Turkey	97	98	49	71	77	47	40	51	44	12	13
United Arab Emirates	90	87	49	82	80	50	39	12	60	13	11
United Kingdom	100	100	49	97	95	49	69	49	57	17	16
United States	97	95	49	91	89	49	105	74	57	17	16

Sources: Net enrollment ratios in primary and secondary education from UNESCO Institute for Statistics (2011a); girls' share of primary and secondary enrollments from UNESCO Institute for Statistics (2011c); girls' share of secondary enrollments from UNESCO Institute for Statistics (2011c); gross enrollment ratio in tertiary education and women's share of tertiary enrollment from UNESCO Institute for Statistics (2011e); school life expectancy from UNESCO Institute for Statistics (2011d).

Note: NA, data not available.

near-universal prerequisite for attending college or university. In many countries, childhood education is compulsory and highly structured through public and private elementary and secondary schools. In addition, outside formal school settings, parents may—to the extent they are able—invest in educational enrichment. In China, India, Japan, and South Korea, for example, some parents send their children to "cram schools" (also known as "coaching centres") and tutors, where they receive supplemental instruction to prepare for the all-important entrance examinations for university. Access to higher education typically requires completion of formal secondary education and demonstration of some level of academic competence. The better a child's formal and informal education prepares her to demonstrate that competence, the more likely she is to attend university. There are a number of important competencies for success and satisfaction in life that are not measured by secondary school completion and college entrance exams; when considering women's access to higher education, however, these two factors are inescapable and largely determine the educational prospects and attainment of women.

As important as understanding the status of girls' education is to understanding women's education, it is also important to understand the overall status of participation (men's and women's) in higher education worldwide. In only a few countries is access to higher education available to nearly all who desire it. With the exception of the United States, in the world's most populous nations (Brazil, China, India, Indonesia, Pakistan) demand for higher education outstrips the spaces available in universities (OECD, 2013). One must therefore view women's access to higher education in the context of university education as a relatively scarce and highly valued resource. It is also important to consider women's access relative to men's in local contexts, in relation to benefits that accrue to individuals and to society with increased women's education, and in comparison across countries and regions. The picture that emerges is—like the one of girls' education—complex.

Table 1.2 shows postsecondary participation rates for women and men in the five-year age group following from the age of typical secondary school completion in each country. The typical age of secondary school completion in Japan is 18; table 1.2 shows that 55% of women and 62% of men aged 19 to 24 are enrolled in some form of postsecondary education. In several countries the proportion of either gender that participates in higher education is very low (e.g., 3% of women and 5% of men in Kenya; 5% of women and 6% of men in Pakistan). But in South Korea, a high percentage of young adults (85% of women and 121% of men) in the relevant age group are enrolled in postsecondary education of some form.

TABLE 1.2
Postsecondary participation rates by gender

Country	Women (%)	Men (%)
Australia	87	65
Canada	69	51
China	24	25
India	13	19
Indonesia	22	23
Italy	77	55
Japan	55	62
Kenya	3	5
Pakistan	5	6
South Korea	85	121
United Arab Emirates	39	12
United Kingdom	69	49
United States	105	74

Source: UNESCO Institute for Statistics (2011b).
   Note: Participation in advanced degree programs results in counting some individuals more than once, which can result in a participation rate greater than 100%.

This calculation includes duplicate counting of individuals in advanced degree programs, resulting in a participation rate greater than 100% in a few cases.

Martin Trow (1974) discussed access to US higher education in the twentieth century as moving from elite, to mass, to universal. For better or for worse, this concept has taken firm hold in international scholarship on higher education (see Trow, 2010, for Michael Burrage's assemblage and critical evaluation of Trow's collected writings). There are no specific metrics associated with the concept (i.e., there are no strict proportions of the eligible population that must attend university for a society to rate as providing "elite," "mass," or "universal" higher education), but as an intuitive concept, it provides common-sense language for understanding the general state of access to higher education in specific national, regional, or cultural contexts.

When less than 5% of a nation's youth have in-country access to tertiary education, it seems sensible to conclude that access is reserved for a relative elite— educational, financial, social, or cultural. Under these conditions, inequities based on intersections of class, gender, caste, race, ethnicity, and religion may be particularly likely to emerge, especially when remembering that access to higher education depends in large part on the aggregate effects of these factors (Klasen, 2006; McDaniel, 2010, 2012). It is impossible to fully disentangle these effects, though improving gender equality in education at all levels is clearly a goal for governments, nongovernmental organizations, activists, and individuals. There may be economic, human rights, or other motivations, but around the world, gender and access to education receive much attention.

Women's Colleges and Universities

Educating women in institutions separate from men is one way to go about providing access. It is not the most common choice in the world—most institutions are coeducational and most women who have a choice opt to attend university with men—but it is common enough that there are thousands of women-only colleges and universities across the globe, with over 2,500 in India alone (Radha, 2011). In some regions such as North America and Europe, women's colleges have their roots primarily in elite traditions of private higher education in the nineteenth and twentieth centuries (see Horowitz, 1984, 1994; Kodate et al., 2010; Rowold, 2010; Thelin, 2011). In other regions, such as East and Southeast Asia, women's institutions also emerged to serve less privileged populations, sometimes through the efforts of Christian missionaries whose primary goal was to convert souls rather than to cultivate women's minds (Feng, 2009; Ishii, 2004; Jayaweera, 1997b; Kodate et al., 2010; Singh, 2000). For reasons related to regional cultures and the history of higher education as a whole in South and Central America, women's universities have not been a visible sector there, though all-women teacher-training institutions have historically been (Purcell, Helms, & Rumbley, 2005). It is impossible at this time to calculate the proportion of all college students in the world who attend women's institutions or the percentage of all colleges and universities that educate only women. But it is fair to say that women's colleges and universities have played a role in opening higher education to women in much of the world.

That role has often been fraught in debate about the place of women in society. In many circumstances, women's colleges and universities have been controversial at their founding. In times and places where men's higher education was well established and women were excluded from it, opening a women's institution challenged the idea that women did not belong in the university (Bailey, 2001; Batson, 2008; Karlekar, 1986; Miller-Bernal, 2006; Palmieri, 1995; Qureshi & Rarieya, 2007; Spender, 1987). During times and in places that had already established coeducational higher education, opening a women's institution challenged the status quo, raising questions about what was not working and that required a novel, single-gender approach (Hasan, 2008; Indiresan, 2002). Even in the twenty-first century, questions about the efficacy of coeducation for women's learning remain (see Indiresan, 2011; Kinzie, Thomas, Palmer, Umbach, & Kuh, 2007; Kodate et al., 2010), and answers to these questions form the rationale for the continuation of women's colleges in regions where they are a small minority of institutions (e.g., Africa, Australia, East Asia, Europe,

North America). In the United States, for example, fewer than forty-five women's colleges remain (www.womenscolleges.org), and they are distinctly countercultural, attracting less than 3% of all female college applicants (Ash & Boyd, 2012; Biemiller, 2013). The choice to attend a women's college goes against the coeducational norm at all levels of education in the United States. As I describe in the next section and in chapters 3–7, these countercultural institutions play a number of roles in women's development as individuals and gender empowerment more broadly.

Having settled, in nearly all the world, debates about whether women belong in college—the consensus is that they do—there are two common arguments against women's colleges in the twenty-first century. Empirical evidence for these arguments is rare, and it is difficult even to find full articulations of them. I therefore outline the two arguments here, drawing from Harwarth and Fasanelli (1997), Indiresan (2002), and Miller-Bernal (2011), scholars of women's education who have summarized contemporary arguments against women-only colleges.

The first argument against women's colleges today is that students at women-only institutions will not learn how to thrive in a co-gendered world. Not quite the same as nineteenth- and twentieth-century arguments that educating women would "unfit" them for their roles as wives and mothers (see Solomon, 1985), this argument holds that educating women without men will ill prepare them for postcollege life in industry, business, or government. Students at women's colleges, critics argue, will miss opportunities to learn to compete with men, to have casual male friends, and otherwise to function fully in a society dominated by men and shaped around masculine norms and desires.

A second argument against separate colleges for women comes from advocates for gender equality who believe that gender segregation, even for the purpose of educating women, is not the most effective route to equality. Keeping women separate means that college men will miss opportunities to develop friendships with educated women, and women will lack access to networks of power that are necessary for postcollege success. The existence of women's colleges in some regions works as an argument against admitting women to colleges that remain for men only; there is no need to open men's colleges to women, the argument goes, when they have institutions of their own. Critics of women's institutions also argue that historically women's college curricula were often skewed toward traditional "women's" subjects (teaching, homemaking, languages), resulting in insufficient opportunities for contemporary students to access the highest-quality education in STEM and other "men's" subjects (business, law, medicine). Women thus receive educations inferior to what they would receive at coeducational institutions. None of these arguments is fully without merit, though it is difficult to locate a scholar, educator, or policymaker in the twenty-first century who is on record advancing them.

But scholars, educators, policymakers, and other advocates are on record in support of keeping women's colleges and universities as a viable sector in higher education. Students and alumnae from a number of countries are visible online in blogs and social media, and the overwhelming majority of their posts describe favorable experiences or outcomes that their authors attribute to the all-women environment. Institutional leaders appear in more formal venues such as editorial columns, also now widely available online. It is not surprising that students, alumnae, and presidents defend women's colleges. Their loyalty is seemingly bred at least in part from having made the countercultural choice to attend or lead one. In a world in which "women's" is often read as inferior to "men's" (or even coeducational), it is necessary to justify the choice to attend, work at, or ask for resources to support an institution that is for women only. In the competitive marketplace for college admissions that exists in some countries, it is particularly important to define and describe the benefits of women's colleges and universities to a skeptical—or indifferent—public. Thus advocates for these institutions must make themselves and their case visible in the noisy, colorful, multimedia milieu of contemporary global higher education.

Advocates for women's colleges and universities rely on a body of research supporting the case that contemporary women's colleges and universities produce positive results for students. Early research on women's education and women's college outcomes provided evidence that fueled both critics and proponents. For example, an undisputed finding in the nineteenth and early twentieth century was that educated women married later, if at all, and had fewer children than their less educated sisters (for an analysis of this so-called "race suicide" in the United States, see Palmieri, 1987, 1995). At the height of the eugenics movement, the idea that women from the demographic group that attended college (white, upper-middle class, Protestant) were reproducing at lower rates than their peers without college degrees (or than women of color, poor women, immigrants, Catholics, and Jews) was unwelcome in many quarters.[3] Once the panic

3. The findings—which still hold—that increasing girls' and women's education leads to later marriage and fewer children are seen as a success story in global development circles in the twenty-first century. The irony is clear. A century ago, civic leaders panicked over educating middle-class white women who were committing "race suicide." Today, civic leaders celebrate later marriage and lower birth rates among women in developing countries. To be fair, "later marriage" in some contexts means reducing the rate of child marriage, which is widely held as a laudable goal. A critical observer, however, might see the overall goals as the same: maintain white, upper-class dominance over poor people and people of color.

over race suicide abated, research on women with higher education and specifically on women who attended women's colleges took on less shrill tones.

By the last half of the twentieth century, a distinctive literature on women's colleges and universities emerged. A substantial portion of it was made up of individual institutional histories, which like those of men's and coeducational colleges and universities tended to commemorate a milestone anniversary (e.g., fifty years, centennial). The institutional history appears to be something of a global phenomenon, as examples of the genre specific to women's colleges and universities exist from Australia, China, India, Japan, South Korea, the United States, and the United Kingdom. I read several in preparation for and after my campus visits. These volumes are informative and descriptive, filled with details about their founding, institutional sagas, heroes and heroines, and traditions. They are limited by their nature in their ability to represent women's institutions as a whole or in an objective fashion, as well as for social scientific investigations of the outcomes of graduates beyond some highlighted alumnae of particular accomplishment. In fairness, social science was never the intent of such histories, and the volumes offer rich detail, screened through filters of loyalty and affection for alma mater.

A social science research tradition has emerged that investigates the outcomes of women's colleges and universities, sometimes in terms of alumnae work and family lives. More recent studies also investigate student learning and development, and the experiences of faculty and institutional leaders. I refer to much of this literature throughout this chapter and the rest of the book. As examples, research evidence supports the following claims:

- In the United States, women's colleges educate less than 1% of all undergraduates, yet they produce a disproportionate number of female scientists and medical doctors (Wolf-Wendel, 1998, 2000, 2002).
- US women's colleges engage students more effectively than their coeducational peers in educational experiences that are known to lead to positive learning outcomes, both academic and noncognitive (such as self-confidence, leadership skills, and intercultural communication skills; see Hardwick-Day, 2008; Kinzie et al., 2007; Tidball, Smith, Tidball, & Wolf-Wendel, 1999).
- Women's colleges in India that include "gender positive initiatives" in their curriculum, cocurriculum, and extracurriculum promote academic and personal development for students, as well as influence their values about marriage, career, and feminism (Indiresan, 2002, 2011).

- Women's universities in India address the particular needs of women in STEM fields through curricular and campus climate initiatives (Aliya, Sherin, & Nagalakshmi, 2011; Chandralaka, 2011; Sridhara, 2011).
- Student leaders from women's colleges and universities in Africa, Australia, East and Southeast Asia, the Indian subcontinent, the Middle East, and North America reported that they learned leadership skills and self-confidence through their experiences, and a majority felt that being at a women's institution made a difference in their opportunities to be a student leader (Renn & Lytle, 2010).
- Public policy in Japan has supported women's universities as locations for the growth and development of women for the scientific workforce (Kodate et al., 2010).
- Government-supported women's universities and colleges in Pakistan provide culturally appropriate, affordable access to higher education and prepare students satisfactorily for careers (Nadeem, Mohsin, Ali, & Mohsin, 2012).

Most studies of outcomes are not comparative or international, though a few include women's institutions in two or more nations (e.g., Kodate et al., 2010; Renn & Lytle, 2010). Given local, national, and regional differences in culture, gender norms, and educational policy, it is not always wise to make cross-national comparisons (Mendez & Wolf, 2011; Mendoza, 2002). As Shahjahan and Kezar (2013) have warned about "methodological nationalism in higher education research," however, it may also be unwise to confine research on issues such as student experiences, diversity, and institutional governance within nation-states.

My solution in this multinational exploration of the role of women's colleges and universities is to make cross-national comparisons and conclusions when they make sense in context, but to honor the cultural and political boundaries of nation-states when appropriate. After all, much of higher education policy related to women's institutions is set at a national level and enacted in local contexts. Yet there are similarities in women's conditions that cross national boundaries in expected and sometimes unexpected ways, as will become clear in the chapters that follow.

Contents of the Book

Following this overview of women's education in general and women's colleges and universities in particular, I introduce in chapter 2 the research project I undertook to learn about the contemporary roles of these institutions. I describe my research process and provide portraits of each of the thirteen campuses I included in the study. The appendix includes more of the technical details1 of my methodology for readers who are interested. In chapters 3–7, I discuss the five overarching roles that I found women's colleges and universities serving. They provide access for women to higher education (chap. 3). They create welcoming campus climates for women's learning and development (chap. 4). They are crucibles for developing women into leaders (chap. 5). They engage in activities for gender empowerment of students and communities (chap. 6). And they act as symbols of women's potential even while embodying some contradictions and paradoxes (chap. 7). In the final chapter (chap. 8), I look ahead to suggest what roles women's colleges and universities might play in the coming years.

CHAPTER TWO

Exploring the World of Contemporary Women's Colleges and Universities

I undertook this project to understand better the roles of women's colleges and universities in global context. Why do they exist in the twenty-first century, and are they necessary in a global system of higher education that is overwhelmingly coeducational? I sought to answer these questions by conducting site visits to thirteen institutions I deemed to be representative in some way of women's higher education worldwide. In this chapter I briefly describe how I went about my study and introduce the thirteen institutions I visited between February 2009 and June 2011.

My Research Process

To investigate the question *What roles do women's colleges and universities play in a global context in the twenty-first century?*, I designed a study that would allow me to see campuses in local contexts, to meet institutional leaders and faculty, and to talk with students about their experiences. Readers who are interested in a more detailed discussion of my theoretical and research approaches should turn to the appendix.

Campus Selection

I am often asked how I selected, out of all of the women's institutions in the world, the countries and colleges examined in this study. Theoretical and practical considerations guided my decisions. From a research design standpoint, it was important to be deliberate in my choices (Miles, Huberman, & Saldaña, 2013). I decided to create a purposeful sample in which I varied nations, regions, and institutional characteristics. I relied on Purcell, Helms, and Rumbley's (2005) compilation of information about international women's universities and colleges and a pilot study I conducted through the Women's Education Worldwide (WEW)[1] organization as a starting point for understanding the diversity and overall distribution of institutions worldwide. I aimed for geographic distribution as well as cultural, political, and educational diversity within regions; I ended up doing thirteen formal campus visits in ten nations (Australia, Canada, China, India, Italy, Japan, Kenya, South Korea, United Arab Emirates, and the United Kingdom) on five continents (Africa, Asia, Australia, Europe, and North America).[2] I also toured a number of other women's campuses and met informally with institutional leaders in cities in which I conducted the formal site visits in India, Japan, South Korea, the UAE, and the United Kingdom.

In considering institutional characteristics for the site visits, I took into account geographic region and institutional differences such as size, age, mission, funding, and control. Women's institutions around the world range in size from a few dozen students (African Rural University in Uganda) to over 40,000 on one campus (Princess Nora bint Abdulrahman University in Saudi Arabia) and over 70,000 on multiple campuses of one university (SNDT Women's University in India). A few (Mount Holyoke and Wesleyan Colleges) in the United States are over 175 years old, and new institutions are opening to meet ongoing needs for women's education (Asian University for Women in 2006 in Bangladesh and African Rural University in 2009 in Uganda). Asian Women's Leadership University is scheduled to open in Malaysia in 2015, and plans are underway to open Indira Gandhi National University for Women, India's first national women's university. Similar to the coeducational sector, women's postsecondary education spans the range of institutional missions from technical degree programs to agriculture, teacher training, liberal arts, and STEM. I sought institutions representing different funding models from fully state funded (charging no tuition or fees to students) to fully private (receiving no public funding, dependent on student tuition and fees, grants, fundraising, and endowment income). Governance and control of higher education institutions vary worldwide, and I sought institutions that represented arrangements typical for their nation. The resulting set of institutions, as will be clear in the site descriptions in this chap-

1. First brought together in 2004 by the presidents of Mount Holyoke and Smith Colleges in the United States, WEW is a loose organization of and for women's colleges and universities around the world. The group has gathered every other year as institutional leaders and has sponsored conferences for students and for faculty of member institutions. Information is available at the WEW website: www.womenseducationworldwide.org.

2. For some time, I along with other scholars of women's higher education searched unsuccessfully for evidence of a women's postsecondary institution in Central or South America. A recent Internet search, conducted after my campus visits concluded, yielded the website of the Universidad Femenina del Sagrado Corazón in Lima, Peru. I welcome readers' suggestions for additional institutions that could be included in a future study.

ter, represent a diversity of case studies in single-gender higher education. Of course, there are thousands of institutions I did *not* visit, and the themes I discuss in subsequent chapters might have differed if I had made other choices.

From a practical standpoint, as a female researcher from the United States traveling alone, I elected not to visit institutions in countries in which the United States had active military operations (e.g., Afghanistan, Iraq, and Pakistan) or that were engaged in their own civil unrest at the time (Sudan, Uganda, and Zimbabwe). Some of these countries are ones in which girls' and women's education is a deeply fraught cultural and political topic (see Kurshid, 2012; Nussbaum, 2004); one could argue that they are exactly the places where women's colleges and universities may be most needed and therefore most interesting. For conducting an international study as a female US citizen traveling alone, however, I deemed them outside my bounds, no matter how interesting and important the findings about the roles of these institutions might be.

Another practical consideration, and one more routine to the conduct of educational research, was gaining access to the institutions and assistance in setting up meetings on campus. In six cases I relied on contacts I made with institutional leaders through WEW. In the seven other cases I initiated communication with the rector, principal, or president, locating their names and e-mail addresses through institutional webpages and, when the websites were not informative, further online searches, including those for ministries of education, conference proceedings, and publication records.

The search for names and contact information (phone numbers or e-mail addresses) revealed substantial variation across regions in the ways that institutions represent themselves online, if at all, and how easy or difficult it is to communicate with institutional representatives. I gained additional appreciation for Purcell et al.'s (2005) first-of-its-kind effort to locate and survey women's colleges and universities worldwide. The amount and quality (i.e., timeliness and accuracy) of information varied widely across institutions, from bare bones "we are here" websites with limited information to interactive multimedia websites with institutional data, staff directories, academic calendars, and translations into multiple languages. When searching for information about institutions for which English was not the primary language, that lacked English translations of their webpages, and that used a language I do not read with adequate skill, I enlisted the help of speakers of the relevant languages (Arabic, Chinese, and Japanese).

Once I had made contact with the institutional leader (variously called rector, president, principal, or vice chancellor), I explained my project and asked to schedule a meeting during the time I planned to be in country. I also asked for the names of deans or faculty I could contact to set up additional meetings with faculty, administrators, students, and alumnae. My requests were most often met with generosity and collegiality, and the planning would proceed from that point.

Methods of Data Collection

Following the concept of a vertical case study, in which the researcher builds a case through exploration of multiple levels of an organization (see Vavrus & Bartlett, 2006), at each institution I aimed to meet with the leader, other senior leadership (department chairs, deans), faculty from different disciplines, and students. Because my professional background includes student affairs administration, I also tried to meet with the person or persons responsible for student services or student welfare. In many nations, student affairs and services is not a professionalized field as it is in the United States (Haddad & Altbach, 2009), and faculty with a full load of teaching assignments would also take on oversight of student welfare, meeting students' out-of-class needs. These individuals were often the ones who set up my individual and group interviews with students. While in country, I also tried to meet with representatives from the ministry of education or higher education; I was able to do so in China, India, Japan, Kenya, South Korea, and the UAE.

I also gathered data through online sources (e.g., institutional websites, student-generated media, news reports in local media), compilations of information about higher education institutions (e.g., public records or private ranking systems), campus observations, and physical artifacts (e.g., publications, flyers, calendars of events). During my visits, I took campus tours and spent unstructured time in public spaces, including cafeterias, canteens, snack bars, and coffee shops; libraries and media centers; women's centers; bookstores; and informal convening spots such as courtyards, quadrangles, shaded pavilions, and benches in corridors. I observed organized sporting events, cultural activities, and a few classes.

I operated on the general principle to always say "yes" when my hosts invited me to take part in an activity that had not been on my original itinerary; I found myself attending an alumna's book signing in Mumbai, marching to "Take Back the Night" with student leaders in Delhi, sharing a platter of homemade pasta with a provost in Italy, observing a sports field day in the UAE, and participating in a Japanese university's graduate seminar on gender in international development. Some campuses were tightly secured, requiring me to sign in, wear identification, and follow an itinerary; other campuses were completely open for me to come and go freely. Still others fell in between. I was asked at one front gate who I was and what I was doing, but once inside, no one appeared to keep track of my activities. As a 40-something white woman in Western apparel, I was an obvious outsider on several campuses, and I was frequently asked if I needed help finding something (often I did). As I have experienced at women's colleges in the United States, students were typically friendly and outgoing, willing— sometimes eager—to help an outsider find her way and to answer questions about their experience on campus.

In the end, data for each site included document and web analysis, interviews, student focus groups, and on-site observations. After thirteen site visits, the data amounted to 198 hours of recorded interviews, 48 hours of focus groups, 3.5 linear feet of campus artifacts, a profile of each institution compiled from online documents, and a database of information gleaned from online and documentary sources about each nation. From these data sources I compiled the campus portraits in this chapter. I then analyzed data across cases following an inductive approach to code and theme development (see Coffey & Atkinson; 1999; Miles et al., 2013). In examining data, I employed both open coding procedures and a priori codes (Boyatzis, 1998) developed from exploratory conversations with college presidents at the WEW meeting in 2008 and a study conducted at the 2008 WEW Student Leader Conference (Renn & Lytle, 2010). Using these coding and thematic analysis processes, I developed the five roles I present in the following chapters: access, campus climate, gender empowerment, leadership development, and symbolism and cultural paradox. For readers interested in methodological questions, I include in the appendix more detailed descriptions of methodology, site selection, data collection, analysis, researcher positionality, trustworthiness, and limitations of the study.

Portraits of the Thirteen Sites
Australia: Australian Women's College

Australian Women's College (AWC) is a nondenominational residential college within one of Australia's public research universities.[3] One of seven residential colleges, AWC offers accommodation and meals, social and recreational activities, and academic tutorials; it does not have its own faculty or grant degrees. Students admitted to the university are then eligible to apply to join a residen-

---

3. In accordance with my commitment to confidentiality for research participants, throughout the book I use pseudonyms for all institutions and people.

tial college, the benefits of which are purported to be both academic and social. The residential colleges at this university are known as the collegiate homes of a number of prominent Australian politicians, business leaders, and other public figures. Residential college acceptance is selective, and approximately 3% of all undergraduates reside "in college." Increasing in size since its founding over one hundred years ago, AWC has space for about three hundred women, or 1% of the university's female undergraduate student population. Historically, AWC has drawn its students from upper- and upper-middle-class white women, but it has begun to have some success in diversifying its enrollment and addressing social justice issues throughout its living-learning curriculum.

AWC students come from any major at the university, in three- and four-year degree programs (e.g., arts, law, social science, medicine, liberal studies), with nearly half in science. AWC provides academic support in the form of weekly tutorials led by postgraduates and university staff. AWC postgraduate or senior undergraduate academic advisors also mentor younger students in their disciplines.

Students who live in college at AWC enjoy the benefits of a private compound of residential, dining, library, and common spaces contiguous with the main campus of the university and adjacent to three other residential colleges. Student self-governance is highly valued, and the elected Senior Student sits on the AWC governing council, a group of external trustees. Student organizations provide a full schedule of sport, debate, cultural, volunteer, and social activities. In the Oxbridge tradition, students once a week wear academic dress for formal dinner. Overall, the college emphasizes academics, leadership, and involvement as its benefits. Students excel in these contexts, and alumnae are both highly successful in life and loyal to AWC, as demonstrated through ongoing connections to the college through an active alumnae association.

Canada: Canadian University College

Canadian University College (CUC) is the only all-female college or university in Canada. Founded in the early 1900s by the Ursuline sisters, an education-oriented order of Catholic nuns, CUC operates now as an affiliated "university college" within a large, public, provincial university. Students are admitted directly to CUC and can earn four-year bachelor's degrees in arts and social science, management and organizational studies, family studies, health sciences and kinesiology, or foods and nutrition. CUC also offers master's degrees in food and nutrition. CUC enrolls around one thousand students, about 90% of them studying full time. CUC has continued the Ursuline tradition of educating women from all socioeconomic backgrounds and offers an extensive scholarship program in addition to what is available through the university with which it is affiliated.

CUC houses about two hundred of its nearly one thousand students, and when I arrived on campus, a new residence hall and dining commons were under construction. CUC embraces a residential college philosophy similar to that of the Australian, British, and Italian institutions I visited. An active student government and residential self-governance are locations for student leadership development. CUC also hosts a university-community women's resource center for students, faculty, staff, and the local women's activist community of the city of 350,000 in which it is located.

The CUC principal came to the institution from a coeducational higher education background. Only the second lay principal of the school, she leads the continued development of the institution as separate from its founding religious order, though still incorporating its foundational principles and rich Catholic cultural heritage. Alumnae commitment to the Catholic institution they remember is strong, and the principal described the challenges and opportunities of working within the structure of the affiliated university (which regulates academic quality and is the degree grantor for CUC graduates) while maintaining long-standing traditions and commitments.

Campus architecture and plans reflect the merging of old and new at CUC. Many administrative and faculty offices, as well as classroom, laboratories, and function space, reside in the original campus building, which sits at the end of a long driveway atop a hill overlooking the affiliated university. It originally included a gated-off convent for the sisters of the founding religious order; this section now serves other purposes, but the college chapel remains intact and features within it a Lady's Chapel, with stained-glass depictions of events from the lives of female saints. The public areas of this main building contain abundant examples of statuary, furnishings, and art that reflect women's influence in the institution's history and the Catholic Church. Students, faculty, and staff are thus surrounded daily by reminders of CUC's founding and commitment to women's education.

China: Women's Federation University

Women's Federation University (WFU) was founded sixty years ago as a vocational school of the All-China Women's Federation (ACWF), the women's branch of the (then as well as now) ruling Communist Party of China (CCP). At the time of my visit in 2009, WFU was one of three women-only institutions in China (one private, two affiliated with the ACWF); in 2010, the ACWF and CCP announced the opening of a fourth, a former branch campus of WFU that was being elevated to independent university status. WFU remains affiliated with the ACWF and is under the academic administration of the Ministry of Education. WFU has made a transition from its founding purpose of educating female cadres of the CCP to an institution for adult education in the late 1980s to an accredited bachelor's degree–granting university that draws its students directly from high school. The undergraduate student population is 3,300.

WFU offers a broad curriculum, including law, social work, management, education, computer science, and some areas of the arts and social sciences. In their first year, all students are required to take a course that introduces them to issues of gender in society. It is the only Chinese university approved to offer an academic major in women's studies, and it also founded the National Research Center for Women's Higher Education. The university partners with institutions in Canada, Japan, South Korea, the United Kingdom, and the United States.

WFU is located on a self-contained campus in Beijing, with easy access to the bus system and a short walk from the metro. Classrooms, lecture halls, library, and some laboratories are located in a central building, with additional buildings providing space for more classrooms, visual and performing arts, and sports. A dormitory houses out-of-town students within the university gate, and a busy, multistory cafeteria caters to students, faculty, and administrators. Bulletin boards line campus walkways and announce social events, preparation courses for the US-based Graduate Record Examination (GRE), and student organization events, including a meeting of what a hand-lettered poster called the "Englis Club" (missing "h" in the original).

Through observations and meetings with the vice rector, faculty, student services personnel, and thirty students, I learned that there is a lively intellectual and student culture at WFU. Yet students reported that before applying to WFU they were unaware of any all-women's institutions in China. Nearly all of them applied only because they wanted to attend university in Beijing and their national exam scores did not qualify them for the public coeducational institutions. Once on campus, students embraced the opportunities for leadership and involvement offered by the women's college environment while also enjoying proximity to collegiate social life at other area institutions.

India: Catholic College of Mumbai

Catholic College of Mumbai (CCM) was founded in the mid-twentieth century by an order of Roman Catholic nuns, at the invitation of Bombay's Catholic archbishop. The original arts faculty was affiliated with the University of Bombay (now the University of Mumbai, or MU), and CCM grew to offer bachelor's degrees in arts, sciences, and mass media. As at the dozens of other colleges affiliated to MU, CCM courses follow the MU curriculum, students take MU examinations, and MU issues degrees to CCM graduates. CCM is rated in the top fifteen colleges for arts. It ranks thirty-third for science in India and second or third in Mumbai (*India Today*, 2012a, 2012b). A distinctive feature is the CCM Centre for Women's Studies and Development, a scholarly unit that supports women's empowerment on and off campus.

CCM sits on property that once belonged to the British East India Company. Its large, pink stucco central administration building on campus was once home to a maharaja. Tiled walks look out through archways to a lawn, garden, and fountains. Located in a fashionable but crowded neighborhood, the gated campus with its palm trees and flowers is an oasis of calm set apart from the car traffic and noise of modern Mumbai. An on-campus hostel houses just over a hundred students from out of town; other students live in apartments or, more often, with their families in the city. A lively canteen with covered seating area is a center of activity, and women in brightly colored saris or T-shirts and jeans sit at tables and laugh and shout to one another. An array of student organizations and sports clubs offer leadership, academic enrichment, and recreation opportunities.

Although founded by a Catholic order, CCM now serves a student body that is only a small minority Catholic or other Christian. The majority of CCM students are observant Hindus and Muslims, as well as women who describe themselves as agnostic or as culturally but not religiously Hindu or Muslim. Some students wear religious apparel (abayas, veils) that mark their faith, but others choose to take off their abayas when they enter campus and hang them on the racks provided for that purpose just inside the campus gate. Nuns and laypeople (women and men) make up the faculty and administration.

India: Elite College

When speaking about my research on women's colleges and universities in India, I am nearly always asked if I have visited Elite College (EC). EC is known throughout India and the world for the quality of its graduates and for its top rankings among Indian colleges for arts, commerce, and psychology. Affiliated to Delhi University, EC accepts less than 1% of applicants and since its founding in the mid-twentieth century has produced a long list of prominent alumnae, including leaders in politics, business, journalism, education, and the arts. Its two thousand students come to EC from around the nation for sixteen undergraduate and ten postgraduate programs of study.

The campus is located in a mainly residential neighborhood in South Delhi, away from most of the other colleges affiliated to Delhi University. To the relief and satisfaction of many students, a new metro line stops two blocks from the campus gate, facilitating transportation to the city center for the three hundred students who live in the campus hostel and for the bulk of the student body that lives off campus with family or in private hostels. In the main campus building, open corridors on three levels overlook courtyards, lawns, gardens, and sporting grounds; flowers grow everywhere in beds, pots, and hanging planters. Unlike at many other Indian campuses, a noticeable number of students wear sweatshirts with the college name and emblem; the majority of students wear jeans or leggings, some with T-shirts, others in "Indo-Western" outfits combining a kurta (tunic) and dupatta (long scarf). Female faculty and administrators dress more traditionally, many in colorful saris or salwar kameez (tunics and loose pants that narrow at the ankle).

In addition to first-class academics, EC offers a rich cocurricular program of student government, clubs, and sports. The student government organizes an array of cultural, political, social, and recreational clubs. Journalism majors produce a variety of student news media; student volunteers run an afterschool program for area youth from poor families; and among a dozen other sports teams, athletics (known as track and field in the United States), basketball, tennis, and swimming teams compete against those from other colleges. Extracurricular activities count as one element in admissions decisions, and the college makes no secret about seeking talented students who excel in academics, leadership, and sports.

India: Urban Comprehensive University

Urban Comprehensive University (UCU)—located on two campuses in Mumbai and one in Pune, with additional constituent colleges spread throughout the region—is the oldest women's postsecondary institution in India and the world's largest multicampus women's university. UCU began humbly in the late nineteenth century as an ashram for widows and "helpless women." With a commitment to girls' and women's education, and inspired by Japan Women's University, the founder opened a college for women, with only five students, in the early twentieth century. Four years later, it became a university and later gained status as a nationally recognized university. UCU now enrolls over 70,000 women in twenty-six colleges, thirty-eight university departments, and eleven faculties. UCU awards certificates, diplomas, postgraduate diplomas, and bachelor's, master's, and doctoral degrees. In keeping with its history of serving adults, it also offers nonformal education and has developed a strong distance education program.

I visited the main campus in South Mumbai, near the University of Mumbai's campus, large public parks (maidans), and one of the busiest subway stations in the city. The campus occupied several blocks, with multistory buildings surrounding concrete or gravel courtyards decorated with a few trees and flowers in planters. The immediate neighborhood contains several other educational institutions, from elementary schools to campuses of colleges and universities not connected with UCU. Carts selling food, fresh juices, and school supplies line the tree-shaded streets.

UCU operates some student hostels, and many students live in nearby private "girls hostels," which range from closely supervised Catholic convent-style accommodations to more laissez-faire operations in which, according to some students, the resident warden seems more like an "older sister" than a "nosy auntie." UCU students organize a host of sporting, cultural, academic, and social activities under the students' union model that is common in India.

Italy: Collegio delle Donne

A component college of one of Italy's oldest universities, Collegio delle Donne (CDD) is a relatively young (30-year-old) public-private partnership between the university and a foundation established for the purpose of supporting a new residential college within it. Around one hundred undergraduate and fifty graduate and doctoral students from a range of academic programs enroll at the college. The college offers courses that are accredited by and open to students across the university, and it places a special emphasis on interdisciplinary learning.

The CDD campus contains living, dining, academic, and other common spaces in which it aims to bring together women from all social backgrounds. CDD conducts outreach to precollege students about college and major choices, assigns a tutor to every incoming student, and provides career counseling and guidance to senior students. CDD attunes its cocurricular offerings to develop women leaders as managers and professionals, including an emphasis on international awareness and competence.

Student culture at CDD includes an active sports association, cultural events, and social activities. A full-time staff member of CDD organizes cultural and public events that feature prominent politicians, business leaders, authors, social entrepreneurs, and scholars of science, arts, and humanities. Students are thus immersed in a context of leadership development through self-governance and role models. CDD is an active member of WEW, having sponsored two conferences (one for institutional leaders, one for student leaders) and utilizing the network of women's institutions to provide opportunities for CDD students to study abroad or attend conferences in China, Japan, the UAE, and the United States. CDD students also take part in exchanges throughout Europe.

Japan: National Women's University

National Women's University (NWU) began in the nineteenth century as a normal school to train women to be teachers, evolving to become one of two Japanese national universities for women. The eighty-seven national universities in Japan are partially privatized but receive public funding and are generally seen as more prestigious than the eighty-nine other public and nearly six hundred private universities in the country. NWU admits only 10% of applicants, placing it among the most selective institutions in the country. Two thousand undergraduates are divided roughly half into the faculty of letters and education, and one quarter each in science and in human life and environmental sciences. A thousand graduate students, half master's and half doctoral, round out the overall student body. The NWU organization also includes prestigious kindergarten, elementary, junior high, and senior high school programs; the young Japanese Prince Hisahito attended kindergarten on campus in the year that I visited.

The campus is in a busy Tokyo neighborhood of shops, businesses, and apartment buildings. It is near other schools—elementary, secondary, postsecondary—and set apart from its surroundings by walls and gates. Students, faculty, and staff seemingly come and go at will. The campus is fairly compact, with little green space between tall concrete buildings. NWU burned to the ground during the Great Kanto Earthquake of 1923, and the present campus grew up along with its neighbors beginning in 1932. A residence hall on campus houses Japanese students from outside Tokyo and international students, who make up about 8% of the student body. Other students arrive on foot from nearby apartments or by public transportation from around the city.

Japanese women's colleges were founded in a Confucian tradition of separate spheres of influence for men and for women, emphasizing the development of the *ryōsai kenbo* or "good wife, wise mother" (see Kodate, Kodate, & Kodate, 2010; McVeigh, 1997; Shizuko, 2012). This philosophy is no longer explicit at NWU, which emphasizes developing women for leadership in careers and civic life. Students and faculty mentioned the legacy of *ryōsai kenbo* when describing a tension they experienced in a twenty-first-century women's college. NWU clearly emphasizes excellence in science and other nontraditional fields for women, and it sponsors a center for the study of gender. NWU openly advocates leadership development, and students have many opportunities to practice their skills. Yet students and faculty described an underlying sense of gentility and tradition that emanated from an institutional pride in following, for over a century, a philosophy of *ryōsai kenbo* that permeated academic and social life.

Japan: Suburban College

Just outside Tokyo's core subway system lies a relatively bucolic suburb of two- and three-story houses, parks, and public playgrounds. A walk from the train station through the woods beside a community recreation field took me to Suburban College (SC), a historic private women's college in suburban Tokyo. SC is named for its founder, who was sent to the United States for several years as a child, returned to attend all-women's Bryn Mawr College, and later went to St. Hilda's College at Oxford University (also all-women at the time, St. Hilda's began admitting men in 2008). Her experiences at these women's colleges inspired her to improve educational opportunities for Japanese women. She opened SC as a private institution in the early twentieth century. SC has acquired a reputation as one of the most prestigious women's institutions in Japan.

SC offers undergraduate, master's, and doctoral degrees from one faculty of liberal arts organized into four departments: English, mathematics, computer science, and international and cultural studies. At the graduate level, SC combines mathematics and computer science into one department. English language is required for students in all departments, and SC takes pride in offering courses at all levels as seminars with ample interaction among students and with faculty. Formal international exchange programs with two-dozen institutions across Asia, Australia, Europe, and North and Central America provide opportunities for students and faculty to engage in cultural and intellectual activities beyond the SC campus. Closer to home, students can take courses around Tokyo through a credit-sharing program with a handful of specialized institutions that offer foreign studies, music, and art.

With nearly three thousand undergraduates and about one hundred graduate students, SC is bustling during the day, though it is much calmer in the evening when most students and faculty walk to the train station and leave behind a few hundred women who live in the self-governed, self-catered dormitories. The parklike campus is compact but offers ample grass, shade, and sporting grounds. Groups of students gather in open spaces, collect around bulletin boards in the corridors, and laugh loudly on their way to class or tennis practice. The setting is orderly; the students a bit less so.

Kenya: Kenyan Institute for Science and Technology

Kenyan Institute for Science and Technology (KIST) is a non-state-funded, secular university operating since 2002 under a letter of interim (not full charter) from Kenya's Commission for Higher Education (CHE) within the Ministry of Higher Education, Science, and Technology. A former senior government official who saw a need for women to receive university-level training in science and technology founded KIST as a private, for-profit institution. Among the wealthiest men in Kenya, he and his family had already opened a girls' secondary school and, perhaps motivated by the experience of watching his many daughters make their way in the world of education, he was determined to create more opportunities for talented female high school graduates.

The KIST campus is split between an urban center and a rural campus. The urban center occupies a few floors of a multistory building, with administrative offices, computer lab, and four classrooms. At the time of my visit the rural campus featured three two-story buildings: one housed the library and computer room, one contained classrooms and administrative offices, and one was a small student hostel. A campus tour took me into the bush to see the location of additional buildings that the founder, an architect by training, had mapped out. The CHE requires a university to have at least forty acres of land at its founding, and KIST's rural campus fulfilled this mandate. While some students might have preferred closer access to urban life, others felt safer and more comfortable in the countryside.

When I traveled there for this study, KIST claimed a total of sixty students but some newspaper accounts that year placed the number closer to one hundred, and Ministry of Education statistics stated 180 (Kenya National Bureau of Statistics, 2011). Such discrepancies are not uncommon among higher education institutions in nations that have not yet developed infrastructure to support more consistent data. Throughout this book, when faced with this or a similar challenge, I rely on my observations and interviews with campus officials and report discrepancies as warranted to describe and analyze the status and role of the institutions in question. Whatever the precise number of students at KIST at the time of my visit, faculty and students reported a sharp reduction from previous years; the global economic crisis of 2008 to 2009 devastated KIST's ability to provide scholarships, and many students could not afford to stay in school.

The curriculum at KIST focused on math, computer science, technology, and business—all fields in which women are vastly outnumbered in Kenya's coeducational universities, where they constitute 10–20% of majors. KIST students study in English, which is one of Kenya's two official languages (the other is Kiswahili). In spite of apparent struggles to maintain enrollment and hire full-time faculty, KIST has actively positioned itself to partner with institutions outside Kenya; for example, with the WEW network. One of the founder's daughters, an energetic leader with a background in business, keeps her focus on ways to advance KIST at home and abroad.

South Korea: Korean Women's University

Korean Women's University (KWU) is one of the world's largest women's postsecondary institutions and one of the most prestigious universities—public, private, all-women, or coeducational—in South Korea. KWU is a private university located in a section of Seoul known for its trendy youth culture. It attracts around 23,000 students from Korea, the region, and the world to study in its eleven undergraduate colleges and thirteen graduate schools. KWU's 170,000 alumnae include an array of female "firsts," including the first female prime minister of South Korea and the first female justice in Korea's Constitutional Court. KWU is the alma mater of 43% of female members of parliament.

A female Christian missionary from the United States founded KWU in the mid-nineteenth century, and it maintains some of its Christian character in the twenty-first century, although the campus is more distinctive for its global, cosmopolitan nature than for any overtly religious sentiment. The university hosts a large number of international students, exchange students, and study abroad participants; 30% of exchange students are men. Courses are offered in Korean and in English, and even the student newspaper publishes an online English edition.

The campus sits on a wooded hillside and features traditional collegiate Gothic as well as modern architecture. Well-tended gardens, benches beneath trees, and grassy lawns attract small groups of students and solitary students reading, working on laptops, or talking on mobile phones. My visit coincided with alumnae homecoming days, and I saw clusters of women of all ages gathered around what appeared to be sites both familiar and new to them since they had last been on campus. Although classes were in session during my visit, few of the students carried book bags or backpacks; one student explained that oversize purses and metallic totes were the latest trend and KWU students, like other trendy college women in Seoul, sacrificed efficiency for fashion. But make no mistake, she assured me, "We take our studies seriously and KWU students are known for working hard."

United Arab Emirates: Middle East Women's College

Middle East Women's College (MEWC) opened in 1989 in the UAE. MEWC is part of a state-funded national technology institute that, at the time of my visit, had separate men's and women's colleges in six of the seven emirates; one emirate had two campuses of each. The campuses operate independently but in cooperation under the larger umbrella of the technology institute. MEWC is one of these colleges. The rector was an expatriate North American academic who had been with MEWC since its third year. He and a vice rector, a female Emirati scholar who made the transition to academic administration, have been involved in the WEW organization from its inception. MEWC leaders initiated partnerships and conferences to bring women's college students, faculty, and staff to the UAE and to introduce MEWC students to the outside world. MEWC is an English-medium institution, though Arabic is the first language of most students. Like much of the professional workforce in the UAE, the MEWC faculty is drawn largely from outside the country. The students, however, are by policy all Emiratis, and they pay no tuition. Although the UAE has a reputation as a wealthy nation, not all of its citizens are wealthy, so there is some financial aid available for students to purchase required laptop computers and to assist with transportation and meals.

A new MEWC campus opened in 2009 in a commercial-residential neighborhood. A modern gymnasium, cafeteria, administration/academic building, and student center surround a central building that houses the library and some classrooms. Carefully tended flowers and greenery bring color to the sparkling white and glass architecture. Palm trees and sleek screens provide shade where possible, though students, faculty, and staff seem accustomed to the sun and heat. Students wear Emirati national dress: a full-length black abaya (robe) and shayla (scarf), sometimes adorned with sparkly trim, over their other clothing. Most students cover their heads with a veil. A few prefer full niqab, covering all but their eyes, and an even smaller number forego the headscarf entirely. I saw a lively badminton game carried out by four women in niqab, no small sporting feat in abayas on a 95-degree day in full sun.

Academic programs run during the day for mostly traditional-age students and in the evenings for somewhat older students. The campus is busy into the evening even though it is nonresidential. The campus is tightly secured; the technical institute's website carries the following notice:

The [institute] is concerned that all individuals students meet are properly authorized to enter the campus. All [institute] campuses have security gates with security personnel stationed at each entry. These security officers will only allow those who are properly authorized to enter the campus. Security officers have the right to prevent female students from leaving the college without permission, *and to carry out random checks on student and staff vehicles. (emphasis added)*

According to the MEWC rector, assuring safety and security is of utmost importance in providing access to students whose families would not permit them to attend without such assurances.

United Kingdom: University Women's College

University Women's College (UWC) is a residential college in the classic "collegiate university" model of one of Great Britain's oldest postsecondary institutions. In this model, UWC admits undergraduate students, conducts tutorials and supervision, and provides academic and personal support as well as housing, dining, and recreation facilities. The university faculties (or departments) set curriculum, provide lectures, conduct examinations, and award degrees. UWC is one of nearly thirty colleges within the university, and it employs fifty-four faculty fellows in over two-dozen academic areas spread across arts and letters, natural and social sciences, law, and human and veterinary medicine. Fellows serve as academic advisors and supervisors, and an additional group of tutors provides pastoral and academic support.

UWC is one of the newer colleges at the university, founded in the mid-twentieth century to create more opportunities for female students to attend university at a time when all but two of the other colleges were all male. Students can be admitted to the university only through one of its constituent colleges. Students apply to UWC directly or as part of a "pool" of applicants to the university who have not declared a first-choice college; students not offered admission to their first-choice college can opt to be put into the pool for consideration by other colleges. As in other parts of the world, young women in the United Kingdom do not always consider a women-only college, and about three-quarters of UWC students end up there because they wanted to attend the university and UWC was the college that offered them a place. The coeducational colleges have lower proportions of students who came through the pooled applicant process. That said, UWC students excel in academics and achieve high academic honors at rates disproportionate to their numbers at the university. Nearly one hundred graduate students who enjoy their own residence on the UWC grounds join about four hundred undergraduates. In keeping with the relatively young age of the college, campus facilities are modern. Architecturally distinctive buildings housing the community areas (dining, library, fellows' teaching rooms) surround a central court with large fountain. Student residences—some of which originally included concrete beds and desks poured into place in the building process—connect by a walkway across lawns and gardens.

The UWC students' union acts as an independent organization to lead student life in college and as a component part of the larger university students' union. Dozens of student societies, sports teams, and social groups maintain a lively cocurricular life at UWC. Attention to diversity is evident through the presence of designated liaisons for lesbian, gay, bisexual, and transgender students, students with disabilities, and international students. A student wiki includes announcements of intellectual, social, and recreational events, as well as opinion pieces about current events on campus, in the United Kingdom, and around the world.

Summary

It should be clear by now that the institutions are different from one another but share some characteristics. There is no way that thirteen institutions can possibly represent the totality of this sector of postsecondary education, but they do provide a basis for answering my question about the roles of women's colleges and universities around the world.

As I describe in the following chapters, I observed five overarching roles of these institutions: (1) access, (2) campus climate, (3) leadership development, (4) gender empowerment, and (5) symbolism and paradox. The roles play out differently in national contexts yet provide a theoretical foundation for examining and understanding the purposes of other institutions dedicated to particular populations (girls, boys, women, men; racial or ethnic groups such as those served by historically black colleges and universities in the United States; religious groups in a number of countries). As I explain and elaborate on each role, I draw examples from the thirteen institutions and ten nations I have just described.

CHAPTER THREE

Providing Women Access to Higher Education

February 2009 was a few months after the global economy started to crash but before it was clear just how bad things would get for the United Arab Emirates. Throughout the glistening city I was visiting rose construction cranes everywhere, but fewer than half of them were moving. Most sat still next to half-built, glass-and-steel apartment or office buildings. My taxi driver had to call a friend to get directions to the women's college campus where I had my first interviews for the international study. He had never heard of it and was—like 90% of UAE workers across all sectors from construction and service industries to banking—not local and not Emirati. When we reached the campus, an armed guard at the gate checked my invitation letter, looked at a list of names on a clipboard, and called the rector's office to confirm that I was expected. He then waved us in, where another staff person assisted me out of the taxi and waited, watching, until the taxi exited and the gate was again secure. Like the city around me, the campus was glistening glass and steel, with trapezoidal screens placed strategically to shade grassy spots surrounding the central library building. Women in Emirati national dress—black abayas and veils, many of them trimmed with intricate beadwork and sequins—walked in small groups along the campus pathways between buildings, their high heels clacking on concrete steps.

Middle East Women's College is part of a government-sponsored technology institute with men's and women's campuses across the UAE. It plays a specific role in national-level plans for economic development and Emiratisation, the process of increasing the percentage of the public and private sector workforces who are Emiratis. The MEWC curriculum is therefore focused on degree, certificate, and diploma programs that prepare Emirati women for work in education, business, health sciences, and other applied fields. A separate national university offers liberal arts programs, though the focus on fields related to workforce participation is clear there also.

Most of the students I met in focus groups, classes, and casual conversations came to MEWC directly after high school and had ambitions that required a college education: Nawala wanted to work in television, Sabirah was training to be a pharmacist, Zahirah planned to be an early childhood educator. In the United States, I thought, these students might be considered "traditional," though that label hardly seemed appropriate in a country where higher education was only about a generation old. In that sense, all MEWC students I met were "nontraditional"—few had parents who had gone to college, none had mothers working outside the home, and career aspirations for a 19-year-old woman were a break with centuries-old traditions in the region.

After we talked for a bit, Zahirah, the quietest of the group, opened up and told me about her goals:

> *My family is not wealthy like some of the other girls. My father is a teacher, and that is why I want to be a teacher also. My mother does not want me to be a teacher. She thinks that I should not work, that I should not go to college, that girls do not need to do these things . . . I think that for the future of my country, it is important that girls and boys go to college, learn how to do something, and go to work. This is what we are told in [elementary and secondary] school and I think it is true.*

Zahirah convinced her father that she should be allowed to go to college to become a teacher, like him. She is the youngest of five daughters and two sons, and the first child in her family to go to college. In spite of their father being a teacher, three of her sisters and both of her brothers stopped school after sixth grade. A high school teacher helped Zahirah learn about MEWC's early childhood education program and scholarships to help pay for expenses not covered by government-paid tuition. The teacher also helped her convince her father that MEWC would be a safe place for his daughter to study.

I met Sameena the next evening. She was a returning adult learner who had entered the workforce out of high school as a secretary for her husband's company. He passed away suddenly, leaving her widowed with two young children. She kept her job as a secretary, but now that her children were in high school, she had decided to prepare for a career change.

> *With all of the changes in business in the last ten years, I can see chances for growth, particularly in areas like human resource management, which is what I am coming here to get my degree in. MEWC provides the chance for me to get my bachelor's*

degree. My classes are in the evening, and my children can now look after themselves
on the nights that I am here. I am very grateful for this college, because without it
I could not make this next step in my life.

Was she worried about a global economic crisis looming just as she was preparing for a career in business? "I am not really worried. Those cranes over there?,"
she said, pointing to the skyline and laughing, "By the time I finish they will be
moving again and I will be ready to take my own office in one of those buildings."

Without question, the primary role of women-only institutions in history has
been in providing access to postsecondary education. Single-sex schools and colleges for girls and women opened because existing educational institutions—
those serving boys and men—refused to admit them and because coeducation
where it existed was not considered acceptable or desirable for every female student who wanted to attend (Hasan, 2008; Indiresan, 2002; Jayaweera, 1997a;
Miller-Bernal, 2004; Solomon, 1985; Thelin, 2011; Wolf-Wendel, 2002). Access
to higher education for women evolved within the context of larger societal
debates about gender roles.

Coming relatively late to the global university landscape, the United States
offers a modern example of a pattern that is common around the world. Harvard
College opened in 1636 to educate men only; colleges founded over the next two
centuries followed its gender-exclusive lead. In the early 1800s, a handful of educational pioneers experimented with "female seminaries" designed to educate
women as teachers and Christian missionaries. Mount Holyoke Female Semi-
nary (now Mount Holyoke College) opened its doors in 1837, and Wesleyan College (in Georgia) received the first charter for a women's college in 1836, matric-
ulating students in 1839. A dozen small colleges, most affiliated with Christian
denominations, offered admission to women in their coeducational programs,
sometimes in conjunction with efforts also to admit students without regard
to race (Hillsdale and Oberlin Colleges are two examples). Public universities
slowly came on board with what was deemed at the University of Michigan in
1870 to be the "dangerous experiment" of coeducation (see McGuigan, 1970).

There is some evidence that women were admitted to some men's colleges
not out of an impulse toward women's equality, but because the US Civil War
had claimed so many lives that all-male institutions with marginal enrollments
were at risk of closing (see Thelin, 2011). After all, many women of this generation would not be able to find husbands and could not continue to be economic
burdens on their parents. Regardless of the motivation for admitting women,
capacity for women in higher education did not meet growing demand, and a

substantial opportunity existed for single-sex institutions to meet the interests of female prospective students and their families. In response, women's colleges both public and private became an increasing presence in US higher education, offering curricula and living environments deemed appropriate for the minds, bodies, souls, and aspirations of female students. Readers interested in the detailed history of women's colleges in the United States should consult the writings of historians Helen Lefkowitz Horowitz (1984, 1994), Patricia Palmieri (1987, 1995), and Barbara Solomon (1985), among others.

As societal views on women's education and coeducation evolved, opportunities for female students at single-sex and coeducational institutions increased. At their height in the 1960s, women's colleges and universities in the United States numbered about three hundred (DeBra, 1997). When maintaining single-sex institutions became untenable for practical reasons (e.g., enrollment declines) or legal reasons (such as Title IX) beginning in the 1970s, formerly all-male and all-female institutions went coed, merged with nearby institutions, or closed entirely. By 2014, there were fewer than forty-five women's colleges, with some seriously considering changes to their women-only undergraduate admissions policies (Ash & Boyd, 2012; Biemiller, 2011, 2013).

With women comprising over half of all college students in the United States, and succeeding in college at higher rates than men, the argument for women's colleges as avenues of access to higher education must be called into question. The same is true in many of the countries considered in my study. Can a women's institution in the twenty-first century be considered critical to maintaining access to postsecondary education? In this chapter I argue that, even today, women's colleges and universities remain vital—in some cases essential—means of access to higher education.

Scholars (Altbach, 2004; Indiresan, 2002; Knight, 2004; Renn, 2012; Sahni & Shankar, 2012) have asserted that women's institutions in the twenty-first century carry out their historical legacy by providing access to higher education in cultural and political contexts where coeducation remains unacceptable. In some Muslim nations, for example, truly mixed-gender education is in effect not possible, though some institutions do enroll men and women into separate programs. But there are also many regions or communities within regions where cultural proscriptions prove so strong as to prevent families from sending their daughters to a mixed school, though some of them will readily consider an all-girls or all-women context (Hasan, 2008; Indiresan, 2002; Nadeem, Mohsin, Ali, & Mohsin, 2012; Sahni & Shankar, 2012). There are additional subtleties to the case for women's institutions as vehicles for access to higher education.

I therefore parse my analysis of the ways that women's institutions provide access to higher education into three strands: legal or technical access, practical access, and cultural access. There are some regional and national contexts in which more than one of these interpretations applies, and there are a few contexts in which none of them seems to. As the examples in this chapter show, however, women's colleges and universities remain critical to providing access to higher education in some local contexts and therefore also on a global scale. Without them, hundreds of thousands of women worldwide would be denied the educational and social opportunities afforded by postsecondary education.

Legal Access

In most of the world in the twenty-first century, the idea of a law against educating men and women together seems anachronistic at best, perhaps discriminatory, or, at a minimum, restrictive of students' choices about where they pursue higher education. Coeducation is the norm, and there are few impulses toward legal or policy actions that would move to resegregate students by gender. Yet until recently, single-sex public higher education was still legally mandated in a small number of Muslim nations in the Middle East. Until 2009, Qatar, Saudi Arabia, and the UAE maintained full gender segregation at all publicly funded postsecondary institutions. In the UAE, for example, I visited the college introduced at the outset of this chapter—Middle East Women's College—which had a brother institution in the same emirate, as well as peer women's and men's colleges in other emirates. Men and women had separate campuses, faculty, and leadership, under an overall central governing mechanism. According to the rector of MEWC, this complex system worked well to "meet specific educational and workforce development needs in a culturally appropriate context." In the UAE (as well as in Qatar and Saudi Arabia), private universities, both local entities and branch campuses of overseas institutions, were permitted to admit men and women, but government universities—at which students from that nation paid little or no tuition—were single sex until 2009.

The current move to "coeducation" at these institutions is, in some sense, nominal and organizational rather than operational. Qatar, Saudi Arabia, and the UAE now operate universities that enroll women and men but are gender segregated by curriculum, class schedules, facilities, or campus location (see Jamjoom & Kelly, 2013; Lipka, 2012; Naidoo & Moussly, 2009). Some of these gender-segregated institutions were originally intended for women (e.g., Zayed University in the UAE), and others were opened for men and women (King Saud University in Saudi Arabia). Although technically coeducational, women and men may remain physically separate, and coeducation is prohibited at other public institutions operating in Saudi Arabia (Jamjoom & Kelly, 2013).

Given these recent policy shifts, it is difficult to identify any nations where women's colleges and universities are the *only* legal options for women's access to higher education. There are, however, local efforts by some religious and political extremists to ban girls and women from obtaining education. There are also some regions in which single-sex institutions are permitted as a matter of policy, though their continued existence relies on the constant negotiation of political, military, and religious tensions. Students and faculty may become targets for violence, as seen in the 2012 attempted murder of Malala Yousafazi, a teenage activist for girls' and women's education, and the 2013 al-Qaeda attack on Pakistan's Sardar Bahadur Khan Women's University. In the latter case, a female suicide bomber detonated an explosive on a campus bus and additional terrorists stormed the hospital where the victims were taken, killing two-dozen people in total. Fortunately, these cases are few in number. Unfortunately, they have real—and sometimes lethal—consequences for girls and women, their communities, and their families.

If nearly all women in the world live where they can legally attend a coeducational public or private institution, do women's colleges and universities still play a role—as they did historically—in providing legal access to higher education? I argue that the era of single-sex institutions as a means of legal access to higher education has ended except for the unusual, and extralegal, circumstance of extremist control of local conditions. While extremists may control some areas of a country, national policy itself does not prohibit all forms of coeducational higher education. In some nations, "coeducation" means gender-segregated curriculum, facilities, and policy. But women are not technically prohibited from studying at institutions that also enroll men. Women's institutions remain critical opportunities in these restrictive contexts, in part because the movement to gender-segregated coeducation in some Middle Eastern countries has been so recent that the vast majority of seats for women in higher education continue to be at women-only public institutions. As well, there has been significant resistance to coeducation, even when keeping men and women in separate facilities and educational programs (Associated Press, 2009). But the legal and policy landscape has changed worldwide, in favor of greater access to higher education for women, whether in single-sex or coeducational institutions.

Practical Access

If the case for women's colleges playing a role in legal access is no longer relevant in most of the world, a much stronger case for what I call "practical" access remains in force. By practical I mean the ways that women's institutions operate to enable access for students who otherwise might not be able to attend higher education at all or to pursue particular academic programs. In exploring practical matters related to access, I determined that the women's institutions in this study addressed two key factors: academic and financial. In essence, these factors answer two access questions for women. *Can I get in? Can I afford to go?*

Academic Access

Academic access to higher education depends largely on primary and secondary schooling, with additional learning opportunities in the home, neighborhood, and family. In a number of countries I visited, admission to university is based primarily or exclusively on results of a high-stakes national or institutional examination. In others, admission depends on high school performance measured by course grades, grade point average, class rank, and subject matter examinations. Extracurricular activities, including leadership, community service, and sports, may tip the scales in admission to selective institutions in India, Japan, and South Korea and to the residential colleges in Australia, Canada, Italy, and the United Kingdom. Whether by exam score, high school performance, extracurricular involvement, or some combination of these factors, admission to higher education depends substantially on formal and informal precollege educational opportunities for girls. Assuming that a young woman has had opportunities equal to those of the young men in her community—an assumption that does not, as I pointed out in chapter 1, hold true in many regions—women's institutions in some nations play a role in providing academic access to higher education. This argument is especially true in national systems where competition for admission is fierce owing to high demand in relation to national capacity for higher education.

In most of the world, as in the United States, women can and do attend all of the most prestigious institutions. Many families are eager to send their daughters to national universities, no matter the cost in precollege preparation through private schooling, tutors, and cram schools for college entry exams. Extreme competition for admission to coeducational universities keeps many accomplished women—as well as men—out of their desired institutions, even if it does not shut them out of higher education entirely. At the comparatively lower end of the achievement scale for aspiring college students, competition does keep women and men out of higher education. Wealthy families with children who are not competitive for admission in country may elect to send their children overseas, but families of more modest means may find their children left out of higher education.

Women's institutions come into play as providers of academic access to higher education across the spectrum of selectivity. That is, both elite and nonelite women's colleges and universities offer admission to women who would not be—or were not—admitted to coeducational institutions of similar reputation and quality. Though institutional leaders were typically hesitant to state it so bluntly, the reality was that admissions requirements (or cutoff scores) at many of the women's institutions I visited were lower than those at the coeducational institutions generally considered to be their reputational peers.

This phenomenon varied according to national context and markets of higher education. In countries that are far from meeting overall demand for higher education (e.g., China, India, Kenya), women's universities provide a net gain—albeit relatively small in national context—of seats for which the potential competitive pool is automatically limited to half the size of that at coeducational institutions. Men are not allowed to apply, so applicants are competing with, at most, half of the college-aspiring population.

In China and Kenya, single-sex education is far outside the norm (China now has four women's institutions; Kenya has one), and the applicant pool may be further reduced because many qualified prospective students hesitate to apply to women's universities. As noted in chapter 1, surveys in the United States show that only 2–3% of female high school students will consider applying to a women's college (Biemiller, 2011). At Women's Federation University (WFU) in China, all but two of the thirty students I interviewed ended up there because, like hundreds of thousands of their peers, they wanted to attend university in Beijing but their scores on the *gaokao* (national entrance exam) did not qualify them for admission at any other institution in the capital city. Though most had never heard of WFU and did not want to attend a women's university, in light of their academic qualifications, their desire to study in Beijing outweighed their misgivings. Rather than attend a coeducational institution elsewhere, they enrolled in WFU. As one student said, "I did not know about WFU before I was applying to universities, but after my score, it was come here or stay at home and go to [a provincial university]." Would this student have ended up in higher education elsewhere if WFU had more stringent entrance exam requirements? Almost certainly. But WFU provided access to a particular kind of university experience that the student sought: a national university in Beijing.

In Kenya, competition for university admission is also strong, and Kenyan Institute of Science and Technology (KIST) plays a role in access to higher education. KIST, a private institution just 7 years old when I arrived, offered admission to some students who did not meet the academic cutoff for admission to the public national universities. In Kenya, about two-dozen private institutions compete with one another while embedded in a larger higher education system where the seventeen more affordable public institutions are far from meeting demand. They do so in a context of systemic gender inequity in Kenyan society generally and in higher education specifically (Onsongo, 2011). KIST sits at this nexus of competition for seats in higher education and a desire to address gender equity.

Kenya's assistant minister for higher education described a gender-based affirmative action policy that had increased the number of women able to meet academic qualifications for the public universities. To be qualified for admission, men were required to achieve a score of 65 on the national secondary exit exam; the score was lowered for women to 63, which achieved a 20% increase in the number of women qualifying for admission. Sometime after my visit, the score for women was raised to 64. Onsongo (2011) offered a detailed description of gender inequity in Kenya public university admissions, arguing that "the lower cut-off point admission to university intervention does not enhance female students' access to university education because it does not address the underlying causes of poor performance in secondary school examinations and does not offer financial assistance to students from poor backgrounds" (p. vii). She argued that the affirmative action policy did not offset the convergence of inferior precollege education, gender, and social class.

Even with affirmative action, competition for admission remained stiff and women did not make up 50% of the student population at public universities. Proportional to their enrollment, they were overrepresented in humanities and social sciences, and underrepresented in STEM fields (Onsongo, 2011). As a science- and technology-focused women's university, KIST occupied an educational niche, one feature of which was that it would admit students who were not academically qualified for the public universities (it also offered other features that contributed to access, which I describe below). The vice chancellor stated, "We take girls who might not get into Kenyatta [University], but they are able to do the work." A student reflected that she was "blessed to have this chance to go to university, because I could not go elsewhere with my 62," referring to her point score on the secondary exit exam. KIST provides academic access to women who would otherwise not go to college.

The higher education system in India is also strapped in terms of finding places for qualified students, and demand far exceeds supply. India has the largest number of women's colleges and universities of any nation (rising from 1,578 in 2000–2001 to 2,565 in 2008–9, according to the Government of India [2010–11]), yet some high school students still see women's colleges as less desirable than their coeducational counterparts, a condition that could result in reduced competition (and thus lowered admissions standards and more access for women who do apply) at these institutions. The two Indian colleges I studied—Catholic College of Mumbai (CCM) and Elite College (EC)—can hardly be considered as means of broadening academic access to higher education. They each admit less than 1% of qualified applicants and do not compromise academic standards in comparison to coeducational or men's colleges in India. But Urban Comprehensive University (UCU), a conglomerate of twenty-six colleges and 70,000 students on three campuses, has a history of serving Indian women from disadvantaged backgrounds as well as a continuing practice of adult education and vocational training. Depending on the college and academic program within UCU, admission may remain highly competitive, as it is for other public universities in India, but some applicants who would because of their academic backgrounds not be admitted to comparable coeducational universities are offered opportunities to matriculate here. "It is our historic role," one academic dean told me, "to see that women who might otherwise be left out have this opportunity, especially adult women who did not get a chance in the first place." For adult students in particular, UCU provided academic access otherwise not available.

In Japan and South Korea, as in the United States, the tradition of single-sex education was of long standing, and the women's institutions I visited there had historical prestige. The rectors, faculty, and even some students told me, however, that because coeducation is so strongly preferred, applicant pools for these universities were smaller than for comparably prestigious coeducational institutions located nearby. Many women were admitted to the women's colleges and universities who would not have made the academic cut at the coeducational institutions. "Yes, we do take some students who are not at the very top, but still we are highly selective in our admission," said a faculty member at one of the two Japanese institutions in this study. Access to higher education itself was not limited to women's colleges, but access to elite colleges and universities in pre-ferred locations was limited practically by students' academic backgrounds or scores on national exams.

Even at the South Korean university, which ranks among the top institu-tions in the country regardless of the gender of the student population, aca-demic leaders noted that students who matriculated there who did not get into coeducational universities of similar ranking. An academic dean told me, "I find it troublesome that all talented women cannot make their way into Seoul National [University], but we benefit when students come here instead. And in the way that we educate them, I think that they benefit also." A student was less sanguine, stating, "Although I study very hard, I did not make the score that I hope on the *suneung* [College Scholastic Ability Test]. I could still come to Korean Women's University, but it was not my first dream." Across the world, a British student echoed this sentiment, saying, "I didn't apply to UWC, but when I got an offer here out of the [general] pool, I said yes. I really wanted to be at [this uni-versity], even if I had to end up with all girls." Even given these two students' dis-appointment at their circumstances, I argue that in China, India, Japan, Kenya, South Korea, and the United Kingdom gender expanded access to higher educa-tion for women, because if these students were men with the same admissions profiles, they might not have had the option of attending university in Beijing, Delhi, Mumbai, Nairobi, Seoul, or Tokyo—or, in the case of the British student, the world-renowned institution of her choice.

The institutions in my study provided academic access in another way. Some of them offered unique degree programs that students could not undertake at coeducational institutions. If a woman in China wants to be a women's studies undergraduate major, for example, she must attend WFU. Among over eighty affiliated colleges of Delhi University (EC is one), home science is offered at only one (a women's college, not EC) and a bachelor's degree in elementary education is available at only seven (all women's colleges, including EC). Leaving aside the question of men's access to studying these fields and whatever ways these majors may conform to and reinforce gendered expectations, women who want to pur-sue these majors have no choice but to attend a women's college. Access to a spe-cific curriculum is a narrowly defined contribution, but for the students seeking these majors, women's colleges and universities provide it.

Financial Access

Providing academic access to higher education is one means of increasing prac-tical access for women. Financial access is another practical concern. As in the United States, where women's colleges serve a larger proportion of needy students than do their coeducational peers (Fischer, 2008), women's institutions in some other countries play a role in financial access to higher education. According to the rector of MEWC, for example, one-third of students come from poor families or families of modest means. Attending one of the government-sponsored women's colleges or gender-segregated institutions is the only viable financial option for these students. Without this option, they would have no access to higher education. One MEWC student remarked, "The college even gave me money to buy the laptop that is required for my attendance. My family was so surprised!"

In other national contexts, financial aid and scholarships provided by the women's institutions put higher education within reach. Scholarships for Aboriginal women in Australia opened doors to the women's college within the university, as did scholarships for returning adult students at a women's college in the United Kingdom. An Australian Aboriginal student leader commented that the scholarship from the residential college made it affordable for her to leave her community to study:

> And now I see other girls at home and tell them that it's true—they really can go
> to uni[versity]. There are ways to pay for it. They see me doing it, and I want them to
> do it too.

The Italian college also reserved spaces free of charge or subsidized them for talented women from modest means.

At UCU in India, affordable tuition, scholarships, and academic programs that incorporated work with learning made it possible for women in a range of economic circumstances to attend formal and informal courses of study. Similar schemes might be available to men and women at coeducational institutions in these countries, but I argue that the particular emphasis on setting aside resources for women (Australia, Italy, the United Kingdom) and on designing academic programs so that women could afford them while tending to their household responsibilities (India) represent gendered opportunities for financial access to higher education. "I come to class in the evening after I work, and my older daughter watches the younger ones. Otherwise, I could not come here," said one woman at UCU. The convergence of gender, family background, and social class circumscribes aspirations for and access to higher education. Efforts by women's institutions to address these intersections contribute to increasing access for women.

Cultural Access

If women's colleges and universities essentially no longer provide access to women who otherwise would by law or policy have none, and if a limited argument can be made for their contribution to practical access, is there any remaining claim to be made for them as critical venues for access to higher education? I maintain that there is. In some regions where coeducational higher education is legal and where women have practical (financial and academic) resources to attend any university, there still remain substantial cultural barriers to women's access. Where higher education is legally coeducational but culturally segregated, women's institutions provide access to students who would not choose, or whose families would not permit, coeducation (see Indiresan, 2002; Kaushik, Kaushik, & Kaushik, 2006; Knight, 2004). Religious conservatism—Christian, Hindu, and Muslim alike—appears to play a substantial role in this phenomenon, though it is not the only factor.

Cultural barriers to coeducation are perhaps most visible in the Middle East, where public institutions remain gender segregated. Students at MEWC would be able, if their families could afford it and would permit it, to attend coeducational private universities in the city. But to many students and families, coeducation remains culturally and religiously questionable. Though the UAE has a reputation as a modern nation engaged in global commerce, and Abu Dhabi and Dubai are hubs for branch campuses of foreign universities, MEWC students "would not be able to attend higher education unless there was a single-sex option that was seen as physically, morally, and culturally safe," according to the rector. To address students' safety, for example, the MEWC campus is secured, as I noted earlier, by tall fences, locked gates, careful monitoring of visitors, and rules that forbid students from leaving campus during the day. The rector stated that parents and husbands who might not otherwise permit women to attend higher education find these measures reassuring. Students were not troubled by these restrictions, and one stated that she was happy for the rules that kept her on campus, because without them she would likely leave "to go shopping." Another student expressed gratitude for the safety measures because she would not consider attending an institution that lacked them. Even the gender-segregated public university for women, which sat in the desert a short drive away from the city center, was unacceptable to her because "I've heard that men enter too freely there, and, I don't know, it makes me nervous to think about." MEWC was the only choice for her.

Some Indian women were also constrained in their higher education choices. Muslim and Hindu religious conservatism effectively eliminated coeducational institutions from some students' consideration. In a study of "pace-setting women's colleges," Indiresan (2002) found that the institutions performed a vital role in access for Indian women. Knight (2004) attributed recent growth in number of women's institutions in India to this phenomenon, stating that rural women's colleges "are the latest innovation and greatly needed to provide conservative religious women appropriate conditions under which to receive an education" (p. 80). Kaushik et al. (2006) made a similar attribution regarding the role of rural women's colleges in providing access. I did not study any rural institutions, but at the urban campuses in Mumbai and Delhi, religious and cultural conservatism restricted some women's options. Conservative families of local women might not permit them to attend a coeducational university, but UCU was an acceptable option, as were EC and CCM for those qualified for admission. A Muslim UCU student in burqa and hijab (headscarf) said:

My parents know that there are boys on campus and we have many men professors, but they did not want me in classes all the time with boys, and I understand that. Maybe when they see that I am ok here they will let my little sister go to a mixed school. I don't know, though, because we have always gone to girls' schools.

Exceptionally talented Hindu women from outlying states reported that they might have been allowed to attend a less prestigious coeducational institution and live at home, but the elite women's colleges (EC and CCM) provided culturally acceptable access to nationally top-ranked academic programs. Their families permitted them to move to Mumbai or Delhi to live in on-campus hostels, which provided curfews, gated campuses, and protection from the outside world. Some students pointed out that, contrary to their families' perceptions, they were free to come and go from these campuses and they enjoyed far more freedom than their parents might expect. Other students living in the hostels reported being uncomfortable off campus and were glad to have the safety of gates and rules. "This school has the number one program in [academic field], and it's all girls, so my parents said I could leave [my rural province]. If it had boys, no way!," said a lower-caste senior student at CCM. She continued, "Even in [my province] they wanted me to go to a girls' college, but the closest one was two hours [away] and the school is not as good."

At the elite colleges and at the more academically accessible UCU, substantial proportions of the women whom I interviewed indicated that coeducational higher education was not an acceptable option for them even though it was the predominant model in India. Some would have stopped their education after high school if a women's institution was not available, and others would have attended far less prestigious institutions near home. In either case, the women's institutions provided culturally acceptable access to quality higher education in India.

Coeducation is also the norm in higher education in Kenya, although single-sex secondary schools are common. According to the vice rector at KIST, some conservative Christian families in rural areas are unwilling to consider a coeducational university for their daughters, thus eliminating every Kenyan institution but one: KIST. Some students reported that although they exceeded the secondary school exit exam score necessary to attend the public universities in Kenya, their parents would not allow them to apply or attend. They heard about KIST through a network of girls' secondary schools (the founder of KIST also founded a secondary school for girls) and convinced their parents that they would be safe. KIST has two campuses, an urban one that serves women who live with their families, and a residential rural campus far outside the crime-ridden university areas in Nairobi. For women from rural villages who had to leave home to attend university, KIST's rural campus offered a physically and morally safe option that was worth paying private tuition to attend. According to one faculty member, "We protect our girls, and the families know that, so they are ok with sending their daughters here to us." Although its enrollment was small when I visited, KIST served an important role in the lives of those students who would not or could not for cultural reasons attend a coeducational university.

Whereas women's institutions in India, Kenya, and the UAE played a distinct role in cultural access to higher education, at institutions in Australia, Canada, Italy, Japan, South Korea, and the United Kingdom, this role was minimal. In these six countries, I encountered few students, including two international students and three recent immigrants, who said that they would not have been allowed to attend a coeducational institution. But women's colleges did offer a less threatening environment than coeducational options for some students who were first-generation college students (i.e., first in their families to attend university); students from rural areas; and students from minority tribes, races, and castes. Some of these women applied *only* to women's institutions, usually in agreement with their parents' wishes. "Oh, there wasn't a choice. It was all girls or nothing," reported a Muslim student whose parents had immigrated to the United Kingdom. Another British student remarked,

It was a big row with my mum. She would absolutely not let me apply to mixed [res-idential] colleges. She said it would kill my father to have me living with boys. So I didn't. I'm still a bit cross about it, but it's worked out.

Because the institutions I studied in Australia, Canada, Italy, and the United Kingdom were residential women's colleges within coeducational universities, they served as "safe oas[es] where parents get what they want—an all-girls college—and students get what they want—boys," according to one administrator.

Providing culturally acceptable access to higher education remains a role of women's colleges and universities. In some nations, such as the UAE, women would not be able to go to college if their only choices were coeducational institutions. In other nations (Australia, Canada, Italy, Japan, Kenya, South Korea, the United Kingdom) the role is much more modest, affecting the small proportion of students whose cultural values proscribe mixed-gender education. India represents the most complex case, in which coeducation is widespread and acceptable to many families, but large communities of religiously conservative Muslims and Hindus strongly prefer—or will only permit—gender-segregated education for their daughters. Indian women from more liberal families can apply to whatever institutions their academic achievement puts within reach, while substantial numbers of equally talented others are constrained to colleges and universities their families deem culturally acceptable, whether that means leaving home to attend an elite women's college or staying home and attending a local institution.

Summary

In the twenty-first century, policy, practice, and culture continue to enable and constrain women's access to higher education. Worldwide, the vast majority of institutions are coeducational, and the majority of women who participate in higher education do so in mixed-gender contexts. Still, there are students who have access to higher education principally because women's colleges and universities exist. At the extreme, women's or gender-segregated institutions represent the only legal option. Women's institutions also provide financial and academic access to particular kinds of higher education. In some contexts, women's colleges and universities fit cultural and religious values that would otherwise keep many talented students out of higher education. Women's opportunities to continue education past high school therefore rest at the intersection of gender, policy, economic means, culture, religion, and personal ambition and academic achievement.

I asked students at each campus some version of two questions: *What if this institution was no longer women only? What if there were no more women's institutions in your country?* And at every campus but one (in China), at least one student said that she would not be able to attend her current institution, and many stated that they would not be in higher education at all. As tempting as it is to believe that all other things being equal (which they are not), every woman in the world would have access to higher education to the same degree as every man in her country, it is simply not the case. Matters of policy, practice, and culture operate to constrain options for girls and women.

Women's colleges and universities continue their role in opening access to students who would otherwise not be able to attend. The relative importance of this role has decreased in the nearly two hundred years since Mount Holyoke and Wesleyan opened their doors. But for the tens of thousands of students for whom the existence of women's colleges and universities enables access to higher education, it is no less important than it ever was. In a global context in which higher education opportunity is not evenly distributed, gender plays a distinct role in keeping women out in ways that are not true for men. To be sure, lagging capacity to enroll all students who could succeed in higher education limits opportunities for men as well as for women, but women face additional challenges related to legal, practical, and cultural barriers to access at coeducational institutions. The availability of women's colleges and universities addresses some of these barriers and remains a critical component of access to higher education worldwide.

CHAPTER FOUR

Campus Climate

Being Ordinary Is Not an Option

My room in the women's college overlooked a fence onto the back windows of the campus chapel at the neighboring men's college. It was shaded, serene, and silent. But a few months before I arrived in Australia to visit this women's residential college housed within a coeducational public university, students from the men's college sparked outrage over a "pro-rape/anti-consent" group they created on Facebook. This incident and the defensive, unapologetic response of the college administration—and the warden in particular—earned the men's college a Gold Ernie award, given by a local group of feminists for the most misogynist public comments of the year (the award is named for former Australian Workers' Union secretary Ernie Ecob, known for his misogynist comments). Although the Gold Ernie made fun of misogyny displayed by students and leaders in the men's college, it also brought attention to the wider culture of sexism, harassment, and interpersonal violence facing women at the university.

The Australian Women's College (AWC) compound abutted the men's college, with a fence and alley separating the two. Historically, the Anglican men's college had been the most prestigious at the university, producing prominent leaders in government, law, and business. Students I talked to at the women's college described the men's college students as "fun" and "sporty," but also as "clueless," "arrogant," and "sexist." AWC students found themselves in a love-hate relationship with their neighbors across the fence. Parties, events, and the student-run pub at the men's college were centerpieces of AWC's social life, but even before the pro-rape Facebook group came to life, there were problems with date rape, sexual assault, and a hooking-up culture in which men had power and women went along with the game.

Katie, a third-year AWC student, relayed an incident from her second year:

During O[rientation] Week it's very common for the new girls to go to parties at [the
men's college], and last year one of our girls got rotten [drunk]. The story comes out
that she went off with one boy, and then he assaulted her and left her unconscious be-
hind a bush outside. Some of our girls spotted her and brought her back to AWC and
cleaned her up. When she tried to find out later who the boy was, no one had seen any-
thing or would say anything. She was embarrassed because she drank so much, and so
she just dropped it. That kind of thing happens more than you'd think. We try to watch
out for the new girls and tell them they need to keep an eye on each other, not take
drinks from people they don't know, not go off alone with a boy.

Other students confirmed this account, which had catalyzed students and leadership at AWC to take some action to educate their students about alcohol and
safety on campus. "Just being at uni doesn't mean you're completely safe, and
being in [the women's] college doesn't guarantee it either," said one student.

The overall student culture at the university brought to mind Michael Kimmel's US-based research on a phenomenon he dubbed "Guyland" (Kimmel,
2008). Guyland, according to Kimmel, is a socially constructed culture in which
young men, starting in middle school and lasting through about age 30, constantly strive to demonstrate acceptable masculinity in order to avoid being
labeled gay or, even worse, unmanly (as expressed by the use of vulgar terms for
female body parts as the most cutting insults against boys and men). If it were
just boys and men in Guyland that would be bad enough, Kimmel asserted, but
girls and women live in this world, too, with two ways to be accepted: be like the
guys (e.g., sporty, beer swilling) or be liked by the guys (e.g., attractive, a willing—but not too willing—sexual partner). In Guyland, everyone seeks the guys'
approval. Students at AWC have their own residential compound, academic community, student governance, and extracurricular activities, but they cannot fully
escape Guyland in everyday life—in classes, socializing, and work.

The fallout from the Facebook incident brought attention to the Guyland ethos
of the residential college system and the university more broadly. Katie said,

After the rape incident [from the previous year] we were all a bit more in tune with
attitudes. But the Facebook group was quite a shocker. For boys who are supposed to
be so smart—they're supposed to grow up and be PM—they were completely stupid to
put that in public. Really stupid. And that's when I started to think maybe it doesn't
even occur to them how stupid they sound. Maybe they really think that it's ok to have
these attitudes about women, or some of them do, in any case. But the rest came right
in behind and closed the ranks. When the warden and the [men's college alumni] got
involved in defending them, that's when I started to think that it's more than just stu-

pid boys in college. They may be stupid, but they've got half of the government behind them. And they will take you down. They will take you down if you try to stand up to them.

Does being in the women's college make a difference in standing up to misogyny? "Oh yes. We've got our own Old Girls. They're not quite as powerful as the old boys, yet, but we're working on it."

In chapter 3, I analyzed the ways that women's colleges and universities increase access. Here and in chapter 5, I answer a question that follows: *Access to what?* An important part of the answer is about having access to postsecondary campuses that are welcoming to women as students, faculty, and executive leaders such as rectors, presidents, and deans. Women's colleges and universities were created explicitly to educate women. It seems sensible, then, that they would provide an environment that is at a minimum free from harassment and at best fully supportive of women as learners, leaders, and educators. In my visits around the world I found the best-case scenario to be largely true: women's colleges and universities are places where students are free to study what they choose in environments that provide physical and psychological safety in societal contexts that often do not. In many instances, these institutions go beyond safety to provide campus climates that promote women's learning in fields that are traditionally dominated by men. I heard from female faculty and campus leaders about their experiences as students in coeducational environments that were not as welcoming, and I heard from male faculty about their observations of campus climate at coeducational and women's institutions.

Climate for Women at Coeducational Colleges and Universities

To understand what makes the climate at women's colleges and universities distinctively positive, it is helpful to know something about the climate for women at coeducational institutions. Around the world—even in regions where women outnumber men in higher education—the campus climate for women at many institutions remains hostile, abusive, or even violent. In the early 1980s, US scholars Roberta Hall and Bernice Sandler coined the term *chilly campus climate* to describe experiences of female college students (Hall & Sandler, 1982, 1984). In reports of the American Association of Colleges' (now American Association of Colleges and Universities) Project on the Status and Education of Women, Hall and Sandler depicted chilly classroom and campus climates for women. They claimed that in spite of women having recently become the "new majority" in US higher education,

Women undergraduate and graduate students frequently do not enjoy full equality of educational opportunity on campus. Students attest, and research confirms, that women students are often treated differently than men at all educational levels, including college, graduate and professional school, even when they attend the same institutions, share the same classrooms, work with the same advisers, live in the same residence halls and use the same student services. (Hall & Sandler, 1984, p. 2)

Specifically, Hall and Sandler claimed that women were ignored, interrupted, and discouraged from participating in classroom discussions; passed over for mentoring and research opportunities; and discriminated against in extracurricular contexts such as student leadership and athletics.

Because Hall and Sandler based their findings on reviews of literature and campus reports as well as anecdotal information, they received some criticism (e.g., Constantinople, Cornelius, & Gray, 1988; Crawford & McLeod, 1990; Heller, Puff, & Mills, 1985). They also sparked an avalanche of empirical research and individual campus climate studies in the thirty years following the release of the initial report (see Hart & Fellabaum, 2008, for an analysis of campus climate studies). This substantial body of literature is perhaps the most enduring legacy of the original reports. Hall and Sandler got the attention of educators and scholars, directing it toward examination of gender and gender-based inequities on campus. This attention has extended beyond the United States to include studies of campus climate for women in such places as Bangladesh (Rozario, 2001), Canada (Osborne, 1995; Wall, 2008), Nigeria (Odejide, Akanji, & Odekunle, 2006), Sri Lanka (Gunawardena, Rasanayagam, Leitan, Bulumulle, & Abeyasekera-Van Dort, 2006), Sweden (Bron-Wojciechowska, 1995), Uganda (Kwesiga & Ssendiwala, 2006), and the United Kingdom (Morrison, Bourke, & Kelley, 2005) and other British Commonwealth nations (Morley, 2006a, 2006b). In addition to directing attention to conditions for women, naming the chilly campus climate provided a platform for scholarly as well as policy- and practice-based examinations of campus climate for underrepresented racial minorities and, more recently, sexual orientation and gender identity minorities, including lesbians, gay men, bisexuals, and transgender people (for analyses of the genre of campus climate studies, see Hart & Fellabaum, 2008; Hurtado, Griffin, Arellano, & Cuellar, 2008).

So what exactly is campus climate and why is it important to women's experiences in higher education? In reviewing two decades of research on a variety of campus climate foci (gender, race, sexual orientation, ability), Hart and Fellabaum (2008) summarized definitions of campus climate as including "perceptions, attitudes, and expectations" (Cress, 2002, p. 390); dimensions of "institutional history, structural diversity, psychological climate, and behavioral climate" (Hurtado, Milem, Clayton-Pederson, & Allen, 1998); and "current common patterns of important dimensions of organizational life or its members' perceptions of and attitudes toward those dimensions" (Peterson & Spencer, 1990, p. 7). In other words, campus climate consists of organizational features and the perceptions that students, faculty, leaders, and other actors have of those features.

As Hart and Fellabaum (2008) concluded, examining climate involves objective and subjective measures. A campus may have a policy of affirmative action for hiring female faculty, for example, which could be regarded objectively as a positive sign of campus climate. But women hired through this policy may experience discrimination in performance review, promotion, and tenure from colleagues who believe the candidates were hired "to fill a quota" or "took the place of a better qualified (male) candidate." Conversely, an institution may lack policies that have been shown to support female faculty, but women in particular academic departments may experience a positive climate resulting from supportive department leadership and colleagues. Ideally, campuses provide organizational features that are free from bias and then create and maintain gender equity, and campus actors at all levels (students, staff, faculty, leaders) feel welcome, supported, and well treated.

Unfortunately, higher education institutions worldwide have some distance to go to achieve campus climates that result in equitable outcomes for female students, faculty, and leaders. As noted earlier in the book, the majority of women in postsecondary education attend coeducational institutions. Many of these institutions began de jure or de facto as all-male colleges and universities, and their legacy of preparing men for leadership in government, law, medicine, business, religion, and society has proven difficult to equalize even where women have become the majority of students. The situation has not proven much more salutary in institutions that have been coeducational from the start, and some former women's institutions in the United States report lost ground for gender equity since they began admitting men (inequity in intercollegiate athletics at Florida State University is but one example). As noted by Poulson and Miller-Bernal (2004), "Coeducation alone, without a transformation in consciousness, does not bring gender equity" (p. 314).

Negative campus climate for women at coeducational institutions is well documented around the world and includes unequal treatment in classrooms, laboratories, and other academic settings; discrimination in hiring, promotion, and tenure of faculty; underrepresentation in executive leadership roles; and an array of harassment, bullying, hostility, sexual assault, and physical abuse that creates an unwelcome, threatening, or violent environment (Indiresan, 2002, 2011; Kodate, Kodate, & Kodate, 2010; Morley, 2006a, 2011; Najar, 2013; NCHERM, 2012–13). It is unsurprising that women may fail to thrive in such environments. Even when the discriminatory culture is more subtle—constituting what Solorzano, Yosso, and Céja (2000) have called "microaggressions," the everyday, possibly unintended discriminatory actions that accumulate like a "ton of feathers" (Caplan, 1994) to create a pervasive negative climate—it can affect women's self-esteem, academic performance, and aspirations (Capodilupo et al., 2010; Sue, 2010).

Higher education is a reflection of society, and what happens on campus may be no worse than what happens off campus. But in institutions designed to promote student learning and development, to embrace the best possibilities for human interaction and growth, and to be at the forefront of creating new knowledge, higher standards for equity and fair treatment should be at least possible, if not attainable. In the United States, law and policy prohibit discrimination and harassment on the basis of sex and gender, yet the Department of Education's Office of Civil Rights regularly receives complaints from campuses about uneven enforcement of antidiscrimination measures (for a listing of recent cases, see NCHERM, 2012–13). In India, female faculty and students face an uphill climb in reforming campus cultures to be more inclusive and less hostile, taking on "deep rooted gender discrimination" that flows from society onto campus in spite of attempts by the University Grants Commission to have institutions adopt antidiscrimination measures (Najar, 2013, p. A12). In her analysis of widening participation in higher education in Ghana and Tanzania, Morley (2011) found evidence of widespread and serious (in one case leading to a student's suicide) sexual harassment of female students by male instructors. In Sri Lanka, women have achieved numerical parity but not equity in the higher education experience (Gunawardena et al., 2006). Evidence from around the world indicates that female students are subject to discrimination and harassment in coeducational institutions.

Women may be the majority of postsecondary students in some regions, but they still encounter campus climates that are chilly or worse. As Tidball, Smith, Tidball, and Wolf-Wendel (1999) found in the 1990s, women's colleges and universities outside the United States offer alternative environments that are at least committed to the ideals of providing a welcoming, supportive campus climate for women's education, if not free from pervasive societal views of gender. Some faculty and students I spoke with were explicit about campus climate as a reason for working at or attending a women's institution. This phenomenon was particularly true in STEM fields, which have been nontraditional areas of study for women and in which women are somewhat or substantially underrepresented in most countries I visited (see Burke & Mattis, 2007; Charles & Bradley, 2002, 2009; Kodate et al., 2010; Mukhopadhyay, 2004) According to faculty, students, and administrators in some regions, the climate for women in STEM was so hostile at coeducational schools that the women's colleges offered the only reasonable access to these majors.

Campus climate is not only about negative features, however. Evidence from the United States shows that a positive climate for women can form the basis of students' academic, social, and personal achievement (Bank with Yelon, 2003; Hardwick-Day, 2008; Kim, 2001; Kinzie, Thomas, Palmer, Umbach, & Kuh, 2007; Miller-Bernal, 2000; Renn & Lytle, 2010; Smith, 1990; Smith, Wolf, & Morrison, 1995; Tidball, 1989; Tidball et al., 1999; Wolf-Wendel, 1998, 2000). Evidence also shows that the positive gender environment at women's colleges and universities benefits faculty and institutional leaders (Harwarth, 1997; Jaschik, 2008; Thomas, 2008). In the next two sections below I describe how students, faculty, and leaders experienced campus climate at women's colleges and universities and how they understood it in relation to the climate at coeducational institutions.

Campus Climate for Students at Women's Colleges and Universities

In the memoir *A Woman's Education,* an account of her presidency of Smith College (United States), Jill Kerr Conway (2001) remarked on how noisy she found the campus of the women's college, writing: "I also loved the lively, noisy sense of ownership Smith women displayed about the campus. I liked to listen to the spontaneously raised voices of students chaffing one another, or barracking in the heated rivalry generated by intramural athletic contests. I'd spent many years on coeducational campuses without hearing women's voices raised in unself-conscious ownership of place and event. The noise level at Smith was the sound of women in charge" (p. 73). Having spent her career at elite coeducational universities (Harvard, University of Toronto), she was surprised at first by the sights and sounds of over two thousand women so thoroughly occupying their campus. Referring to Virginia Woolf, she noted, "This was not just a room of one's own but an entire institution that its graduates owned, beholden to no one but their female predecessors. It gave women, however briefly, a sense of owning their place in life, a place never thereafter easily surrendered" (p. 57). Former

Mount Holyoke president Joanne Creighton, another "convert" to leading a women's college (see Jaschik, 2008), has also written about the ways that students at women's colleges are empowered: "Women's colleges are not about separating women from the world but about encouraging them to be active agents within it" (Creighton, 2007, para. 4).

This sense of women taking up space and having a voice leads my understanding of the climate for students at the campuses I visited around the world. Students talked about the ways in which they were not only encouraged but expected to speak up and speak out. They also talked about the ways that the absence of male students helped them to worry less about how they were perceived when they participated in class or extracurricular activities, allowing them to focus on developing their ideas and leadership rather than on the intricate gender roles, performances, and expectations that surrounded them at home and in their communities.

If pressed to define a single common element of campus climate across the thirteen colleges and universities in this study, I would suggest that each institution espoused an ethos of high expectation for students, regardless—or perhaps because—of their gender. Students described ways their alma mater expected great things of them academically and personally. In some contexts, this overall climate of high expectations ran counter to what students experienced outside college, where gender norms dictated that they not aspire beyond traditional women's roles. Women who came from families with race, class, or caste privilege may have gotten messages throughout their lives that they could be and do anything they wanted. The women's colleges reinforced these beliefs and raised the bar even higher, for example, by pointing to examples of alumnae who had gone on to be heads of state or corporations. Not one student described gender-based harassment or discrimination on campus, even when I asked directly or if they had "heard about something happening to anyone else." The presence of positive expectations and absence of negative experiences created campus climates for student success.

The climates of these institutions were not without their downsides, including some students expressing feeling "pressure" to achieve and faculty reporting that the institution, while supportive, also placed heavy burdens on women to succeed. High-achieving students around the world succumb to stress, depression, and anxiety; the women's colleges and universities in this study had their share of troubled students, including one who committed suicide off campus during one of my visits. The positive and negative effects of the overall campus climate will become clearer as I describe the climate in academic (e.g., classroom, laboratory, research) and extracurricular settings (e.g., sports, clubs, residences, student governance, social life).

Classroom and Academic Climate

The most important context in higher education is arguably the academic one, so I begin my discussion of campus climate at women's colleges and universities with environments designed explicitly for promoting students' intellectual development, including majors, classes, laboratories, and research. In all of these categories, students reported ways that they experienced challenge, support, and high expectations. They often commented on what they believed would be different about the climate at coeducational institutions, based on things they had heard or read, or in a few cases based on prior experiences at coeducational campuses before transferring to the women's college. Students who belonged to all-female residential colleges within coeducational universities (Australia, Canada, Italy, the United Kingdom) made direct comparisons between the climate in contexts that were all women and those that were mixed gender.

Classroom Climate

In terms of classroom settings, I found substantial evidence of warm and inclusive climate. Students reported few of the behaviors labeled "chilly" by Hall and Sandler (1982). They did not feel ignored, interrupted, or put down, and they believed that their instructors and peers took them seriously. At an elite college in India, "Our professors expect a lot of us girls, and there is no way to avoid speaking up in class. So I'm always prepared." In a business course in the UAE, I observed an expatriate instructor from North America use collaborative learning strategies involving all students in small groups to discuss the recent financial collapse. She explained, "Some of [the students] aren't used to having a voice. No one listens to the daughter at home. They're surprised when I insist that they have something to say and that they say it. We take it in baby steps." Asked to say more about these "baby steps," she elaborated, "It starts with sitting in a circle, meeting everyone's eyes, saying something neutral, like introducing themselves. Then I try to get them to voice facts and opinions based on facts. It doesn't always happen in one semester." The class I observed sat in a circle, on comfortable cushions in the carpeted classroom.

Getting out of the desks seems to help the discussion, too, since they don't feel so
"I am the teacher, you are the student," and the girls who think they're not as smart
can't hide behind the girls who think they are. It's more equal.

This purposeful construction of an inclusive classroom climate differs sub-stantially from a hierarchical, teacher-centered approach where the instructor is the center of power, a center from which she may (even inadvertently) silence women's voices. Of course, not every classroom at MEWC is like this one, and not every women's college features learner-centered pedagogy. But this exam-ple points to awareness on the instructor's part that her students lived in a gen-dered context that rarely expected them to contribute to intellectual discussions. She created a space where expectations were higher and provided scaffolding to help students meet those expectations. "They don't all get there, but that's my goal," she said.

Similarly high expectations met students in lectures, classes, and seminars at institutions in other countries. These high expectations did not always origi-nate in an explicit goal to raise women's self-concept. Sometimes they originated from frustration. Some faculty who had experience as students or instructors at coeducational institutions were surprised by how little their students at the women's colleges and universities had to say, how reticent they were to argue a point or raise a question, how apathetic they seemed about vocally demonstrat-ing their knowledge. A faculty member in Italy wished her students would pitch in and "say their opinions."

> When I teach with the men, there is never a problem with them saying what they
> think. The problem with them is that they say whatever they think, without facts.
> But the woman. The woman may have the facts, but she will still stay quiet. In the
> mixed classes, she will stay quiet. In our [women's] college classes, she will stay quiet
> at first. Then maybe she will see that no one else will say a thing, so she will say it.
> Sometimes it is very quiet for a long time!

Classroom climate in this case was not a matter of ignoring or interrupting women, but of creating a climate that was encouraging and nonthreatening so that they would find—and use—their voices. Having taught interactive classes that included men, some instructors found themselves at a loss for strategies to engage women.

This phenomenon was less troubling to instructors in regions with a tradi-tion of more didactic teaching approaches (e.g., China, Japan, South Korea), but it still came up. "I went to the first day of the graduate seminar and no one said anything. I thought they were not prepared. They were, but they did not know that I would expect them to discuss the articles," said one South Korean pro-fessor. "Once they understood how the seminar would run, they were ok. They understood their part. They would speak and listen [to one another]." The expectations of the seminar ran counter to students' prior learning experiences and to gendered expectations that their role in the classroom was to stay quiet and unnoticed. A Japanese instructor noted, "One day they realize that no one else is there to answer. No boy will answer the question. If someone is going to answer the question, it will be a girl. And [they realize] why not me?" Expectations may therefore be explicit, as in a seminar that requires participation by all, or tacit, as in a traditional lecture-and-question format where no men are present. In either case, women must speak up in class, and, according to instructors, eventually they do.

Climate in STEM Fields

Academic majors and courses of study around the world have historically been highly gendered, with women overrepresented in fields like humanities, education, nursing, and social work, and underrepresented in STEM fields (Barone, 2011; Charles & Bradley, 2002, 2009; Kodate et al., 2010; McDaniel, 2012; Solomon, 1985; Thelin, 2011). Although there have been recent gains in some fields (e.g., business, biological and life sciences), around the world women remain underrepresented in STEM courses of study (see McDaniel, 2012, for a country-by-country analysis). Scholars of this phenomenon have offered a number of explanations for the recent shifts, with reasons including women's preferences for "caring" (e.g., social work and education) over "technical" (e.g., engineering and computer science) fields, gender role norms and expectations, a gendered advantage to girls in precollege schooling, and the influence of international nongovernmental organizations promoting gender equity (see Barone, 2011; Buchmann & DiPrete, 2006; Buchmann, DiPrete, & McDaniel, 2008; Charles & Bradley, 2002, 2009; Lihamba, Mwaipopo, & Shule, 2006; McDaniel, 2012; Mukhopadhyay, 2004; Schofer & Meyer, 2005; Shackleton, Riordan, & Simonis, 2006). Understanding the antecedents of gendered differences in choice of academic field is an important undertaking. But my project was more concerned with what happens once students are in a field. What climate do they encounter within their major field of study?

At all of the institutions I studied, students engaged in so-called traditional women's fields (education, humanities), nontraditional fields (STEM), and fields on the cusp (business, journalism, communication). Of course, what is "traditional" or "on the cusp" in one region may be avant-garde or beyond the pale in another and vice versa. Whether in traditional, nontraditional, or emerging fields for women, students and faculty at these institutions reported positive academic climates—free from harassment and discrimination—that encouraged learning.

A number of women's institutions in this study offered a particular focus on STEM fields. Women have historically been much less likely than men to enter these fields (Barone, 2011; Burke & Mattis, 2007; Charles & Bradley, 2002, 2009; Charles & Grusky, 2004; Kodate et al., 2010; Mukhopadhyay, 2004; Sax, 2001), which are key domains for intellectual contribution and economic development (both personal and societal) in the twenty-first century. Certainly that is the case in Africa generally (see McDaniel, 2012) and in Kenya in particular, where the assistant minister for higher education reported that only 7% of STEM majors in 2009 were women. According to him, the gender gap in college attendance (women represented about 40% of students in all fields) and in STEM fields results from boys' and girls' differential performance in high school; as I noted in chapter 3, performance on the secondary school exit exam determines eligibility for public university admission in Kenya.

According to Kenyan faculty and students, even with the affirmative action policy in place to close the gender gap in college attendance, women who want to study STEM fields often face harassment and discrimination from male peers and faculty. This maltreatment creates a chilly, unwelcoming climate that in turn creates a barrier, if not a complete prohibition, to women's full access to equitable environments in STEM education. When KIST opened with the explicit goal of teaching women science, technology, and business—all nontraditional fields for women in Kenya—the (male) founder hoped that "the girls will see that they can do these things. We want them to do these things. We *need them* to do these things." Asked why he thought that they could not learn to "do these things" in coeducational universities, the founder said,

> *I have daughters. They are smart. They can do maths. But I was a boy at university and I know how boys can be when there is only one or maybe two girls in the class. Not very nice. I wanted to have a place where girls could be away from the boys, where it was not just one or two girls learning science and technology.*

I asked if he thought it was a matter of critical mass, whether having enough girls in a class would create a tipping point at which the behavior toward them would be more civil. "If there is even only one boy, he will be the center, in his eyes, with the teacher, and with the girls. No. I believe it must be completely separate."

Faculty at KIST reinforced the founder's viewpoint. Several of them were male faculty who taught one or two STEM courses at KIST as well as courses at other Nairobi-area universities. "It is definitely different here," one faculty member remarked. "We are careful to see that the girls are keeping up, that they can do the work. At [the other university] it is more competitive, with men racing to be on top and women holding behind." Another faculty member talked about his recent experience as a graduate student in Kenya, where male students worked together late into the night but excluded the few female students in their program. He said:

> *At that time it seemed like we were doing it because we did not think that girls should be staying late at the school, and that is what we said. But why did we not offer to work at different times, or include them in our group? We thought they could not be as smart because they were girls. They would slow us down. Now I see that is not true.*

From "not very nice" behavior to competition and exclusion, men's treatment of women at coeducational institutions shaped how leaders and staff at KIST worked to create a more inclusive climate for students in science, technology, and business. Students reported no poor treatment at KIST, talking instead about how they had access to computers and textbooks without fear of competing with men for these shared resources on campus. As noted in chapter 3, many KIST students were from rural communities and had attended single-sex primary and secondary schools, which are common in Kenya. They may have lacked the confidence to compete in STEM majors, massively outnumbered by male students. In chapter 8, I take up the topic of how well these women's institutions prepared graduates for life in the context of cogendered but unequal societies, but it is worth noting here that forcing women to endure hostile learning environments at coeducational universities for the sake of building their tolerance for abuse that may seem inevitable in the STEM workforce is not an appealing alternative to providing a safe, welcoming campus climate.

In Japan and South Korea, some women's institutions have particular strengths in life and physical sciences, and by all accounts their climate for students was demanding but positive. A Japanese scientist, herself an alumna of the college at which she was teaching when I met her, described the difference between the women's college and the coeducational national university at which she earned her PhD.

> *It is true that we do not have all of the most advanced scientific equipment for doing [my specialty]. We had that at my graduate university, but most of the undergraduates would never use it. Here we give our students hands-on experiences with the equipment we do have, but unlike in the university, when women and men students are together, the men [there] do the work while the women watch. Our students here must do the work, they cannot only watch. Is it better to have nicer equipment and only watch?*

Or to have less equipment and do the work? I think for undergraduates, doing the
work is better. If they only watch while they are undergraduates, will they still want to
go on to postgrad study? Maybe not.

In this case, the "cost" for full participation in the lab was to be in an all-women's setting with less advanced laboratories. The professor, who had experienced both contexts, believed that women did better when they could participate, even if it meant accepting this condition. The college I was visiting was nationally ranked for the scientific field in which this professor was teaching, so the equipment may not have been that far behind what was available at the coeducational national universities. But still, women might have to sacrifice some of their scientific opportunities in order to learn in an environment in which they were expected to participate fully.

The South Korean university was one of the top-ranked research universities—single-sex or coeducational—in the nation and known around the world for producing female scientists. Students compared their experiences with those of their friends at the coeducational universities.

I hear some bad things about the professors [at a national university]. They are all
men, and they do not treat the girls as well as the boys. My friend wanted to work with
one of the famous professors, but he said that he would not, because the girls cared
more about boys and clothes . . . I care about boys and clothes, but I also care about
getting good grades and a good job. I want to work for Google or Samsung when I
graduate . . . My professor knows people at Samsung and will introduce me.

Not taking women seriously is one of the hallmarks of a chilly climate (see Hall & Sandler, 1982; Wolf-Wendel, 1998, 2000). Using mentoring networks to help women reach their academic and professional goals, as this student's professor was doing, is one way to counter the chilly climate in STEM fields (Burke & Mattis, 2007; Kodate et al., 2010; Sax, 2001).

Faculty and students reported that they had witnessed or heard about behaviors in coeducational settings that went well beyond chilly climates. An Indian faculty member recalled an incident during her graduate program in which male students repeatedly vandalized one female student's lab equipment, causing her to fall behind in her work and to be dismissed from the lab. There was no proof that the vandalism was based on gender, but the victim believed it was. The faculty member I interviewed said that the incident "began my commitment to women in [her field]. It is part of why I came to Catholic College of Mumbai . . . I would not say I was a feminist before that. I was a scientist."

Then I became both." Students in Kenya had heard about harassment and sexual assault in university laboratory settings. Faculty corroborated their reports and spoke about creating a "safe environment" for women to study science. They took specific steps, such as always having someone else present or nearby when a student was working one-on-one with a male faculty member. A female dean said, "Our students are like daughters, and we would not harm them."

The particular learning environments of some STEM fields (e.g., laboratories, field studies) posed a potential threat to women in coeducational universities. At the women's colleges and universities, the absence of male students and the greater likelihood of having female faculty minimized this threat, a factor I discuss below. Countering the effects of a chilly climate in STEM education took many forms, from ensuring basic safety and promoting full participation in learning environments to encouragement and mentoring.

Climate in Non-STEM Fields

Students also reported positive climates in academic fields in which women had reached a threshold of participation (e.g., business, political science, economics, journalism). In these interviews and focus groups, there was less talk of avoiding negative incidents at coeducational institutions and more discussion of the ways that faculty supported student learning and reminded women that although they were entering academic fields in which women were no longer underrepresented, they should not take for granted this relatively recent development. In professional fields such as business and law, some students expressed awareness that they were preparing for a career in which women were still underrepresented and might face discrimination in hiring and promotion. Other students seemed unconcerned about potential gender bias in the workplace and assumed that they would be judged on their talent, much as they felt while in college, a perception on their part that I took as a sign of a supportive academic climate.

Women studying business in the UAE provide an interesting example. According to the rector, MEWC sought to provide a culturally relevant education within the larger goals of national economic policy that sought "Emiratisation" of the workforce. That is, with a workforce that was 90% non-Emirati, the government sought to increase the number of Emirati citizens working in all sectors. Emirati women in particular needed to take their place in the workforce, going against centuries-old traditions of gender segregation that kept women's work in the home (see, e.g., Goby & Erogul, 2011, for an analysis of female entrepreneurship in the UAE). Several academic programs at MEWC focused on preparing traditional age and returning adult women for careers in business: administration, entrepreneurship, accounting, tourism, finance, human resources, and so forth. The climate of the business world—and Emirati society in general—might yet prove a chilly one for women's careers (see Goby & Erogul, 2011; Metcalfe, 2011), but the college's climate was one of support, challenge, and encouragement.

Faculty and institutional leaders designed curriculum and pedagogy that accounted for social and cultural realities while also preparing students for a changing world of work. They did so through what one faculty member called "a relentlessly supportive approach." Asked what she meant, she said,

> These women come with all kinds of baggage culturally and educationally. I make
> sure they understand that they can be successful here and in a career, whether that is
> doing bookkeeping for a government bureau or starting their own business.

Students in some business programs ran an on-campus shop that sold snacks, sundries, newspapers, and gifts; the clientele of the shop worked or studied on the gated, guarded campus and was therefore about as "safe" as one could imagine. I visited the shop while I was on campus and asked the student staff about some of the products. They seemed taken aback by a US visitor inquiring in rapid English, but warmed to my unfamiliar presence until I was able to inquire about their experience, which they reported as a "good way to practice" what they were learning in courses. They also reported that their instructors provided support and encouragement, and helped them solve problems that arose in the running of the shop.

Students also ran a long-standing annual bazaar that was open to the community and attracted leaders from commerce and higher education sectors. By design, it forced students to interact directly with people from outside the MEWC community in both planning and implementing the event. It is worth remembering that MEWC students did not live on campus; rather, they interacted daily with the world outside the locked gates, and many of them were not strangers to commerce (albeit as customers at the mall or souk rather than as businesswomen). But being in the position to organize and implement the bazaar (since renamed the Entrepreneurship Competition and Showcase) gave them confidence that they could be successful business leaders. Faculty and advisors "gave us support but let us do the work, they taught us how to be successful, but it was up to us to do it," reported one student with evident pride. Part curricular, part extracurricular, the bazaar was a good example of creating a positive climate for learning in the context of a complicated sociocultural context for women's education and career development.

Different but equally positive opportunities in "threshold" fields existed for students in Australia, China, India, Italy, and the United Kingdom. Alumnae of the women's residential college in Australia held senior leadership roles in government, and students held themselves up to these examples of achievement. "Everywhere you go in [the] college are reminders that you are supposed to be *the* top leader in politics or *the* best one in journalism or *the* best at this or that," a student reflected. Having lived "in college" for a week and seen plaques, alumnae registers, posters, portraits, and other artifacts, I agreed. She went on, "Through the tutors and seminars they push us to get to the top. You feel like being ordinary is not an option." The principal agreed: "We provide the resources that let students make the most of their courses. They don't get lost in the larger university. And we provide that extra leg-up so that they excel as students, not just as women students." Students in AWC were mixed across academic programs (or "faculties"), which meant that they attended coeducational classes in which the climate varied from what a psychology student called "completely fine . . . the girls dominate" to what a law student deemed "sort of appalling—boys take charge and the profs don't notice." AWC supplemented, or attempted to counter, field-specific academic climates with in-college tutorials in more than thirty subjects. The expectation that "being ordinary is not an option" permeated the in-college climate, and the college provided resources and support to help students achieve the extraordinary.

An industrial entrepreneur founded the Italian women's residential college, and her legacy lived on through a similar emphasis on excellence in fields in which women have recently broken through: business, communications, medicine, politics. During my visit, an alumna who had excelled in international business returned to give a talk to students, and a conference brought several prominent female politicians to campus. After the event, a student leader told me, "Having [the alumnae and the public leaders] here reminds us that no matter our subjects, we can do very well in our careers." An instructor of Collegio della Donna courses promoted "feminism in thinking" about postcollegiate work in medicine. She explained,

> *In Italy, a woman may be feminist, but she must also be feminine. We can show [the students] different ways to do this. In truth, few of our students say they are feminists. But maybe they are starting to think that way even if they do not know it.*

A climate of support for academic and professional success also took into account the gendered cultural context into which students would enter after college.

Moving from "breakthrough" fields to traditionally "feminine" fields such as the humanities, languages, and education, the climate remained positive at the women's institutions. A majority female faculty and highly gendered academic context met students' expectations for what they would experience entering "women's fields" at women's colleges and universities. If they lived on campus or in nearby single-sex hostels, they might rarely encounter men in their daily activities. While some students found this circumstance socially constraining—"It's not like I would ever meet a boyfriend at college"—others found it a welcome environment—"I'm just as happy without [boys], because I know that when I leave [my university] they will be there."

Faculty sometimes pushed students in these subjects to think about what it would be like to teach boys in a coeducational grammar school or deal with a male boss or colleagues at work, for example. In China, which espouses gender equality in employment and education, if not in domestic relations, a female humanities professor said,

> I worry that they will not be able to handle [men] in their jobs. So I arrange for them
> to have a debate with men from [a nearby university] in my class. We go to [the other
> school] once, and the men come here once. The women need to see how men act.

In preparing her students for the debate, the professor talks about gender roles and gendered norms in society. "At WFU they have one experience, and they learn that women do not have to stay quiet. We tell them that and they see it here. At [the nearby school] they see the difference." A student who had participated in this activity confirmed the professor's account, saying "I think WFU has helped me become a better speaker in mixed [gender] groups. I do not stay quiet as I did when I first came here." Contrary to the overall trend toward providing increased support for women in academic fields, this faculty member found it necessary to introduce some gender-based challenges into the curriculum. She did so in a way that maintained a supportive climate coupled with high expectations.

Across all academic areas, the climate for women's learning appeared to be positive. In interviews and focus groups, I heard about the ways that students were and felt supported and valued. In informal observations of faculty working with students in libraries, tutoring centers, and labs, I saw and heard faculty treating students with respect and encouragement. From institutional leaders, I heard clear messages that they intended for their institutions to be places where women could study any field without worrying about being ostracized, ignored, or mistreated. Women's colleges and universities around the world seem clearly to fulfill a role of providing positive classroom and academic climates for women's learning.

Campus Climate for Students

An explicit focus on developing women as leaders characterized the campus climate at several institutions in my study. The role of women's colleges and universities in leadership development is the focus of chapter 5. There are a number of other features of campus climate that bear noting here. High expectations paired with high levels of support for students' academic experiences marked the climate for students in extracurricular activities (clubs, student government, arts, volunteer service), sports (recreation, intramurals, interinstitutional competitions), and religious communities. And this climate reflected the spirit that Jill Ker Conway found at Smith College: women expanded to fill the campus space with their bodies and voices.

In a demonstration of campus climate that evoked Conway's (2001) description of Smith students, I observed the way that students "owned" Catholic College of Mumbai, the elite Indian institution located in a former raj's palace. In a city that was densely populated, with minimal green space and foliage, the campus felt parklike with a green lawn, a canopy of tall trees, gardens, and elegant campus buildings surrounding a fountain. Immediately inside the gate from the street hung a row of several dozen pegs. As students entered through the gate, they shed burqas and wraps to reveal brightly colored tunics, kurta, or T-shirts over traditional salwar (loose pants) or jeans. They laughed loudly, shouted across to friends in the canteen, and created a general din. In the garden they slung themselves onto grass or stood with arms akimbo, in animated conversations. CCM students were apparently not self-conscious in this garden oasis within a city known for being hostile to women who act in unexpected or "loud" ways (for an analysis of expectations for women in public spaces in Mumbai, see Phadke, Khan, & Ranade, 2011).

I asked students what it was like for them to be on campus. Students who lived at home in conservative families spoke of campus as "a beautiful place," "a place where I don't worry about what my mother would say if she saw me," and "the place where I can say what I wish." Students who lived on campus chafed at the curfew imposed by the hostel warden, but also spoke of the freedom they had within the campus gates that they lacked elsewhere in the city or at home. In their minds, the contrast was clear between the oasis of relative freedom on campus and the restrictions placed on their movement and self-expression off campus—gendered expectations that were lived out in their bodies as well as minds.

In a different context of setting expectations for women's bodies and minds, the rector at MEWC took a particular interest in student health and well-being, believing that healthy lifestyles including fitness and smart nutrition were as important to women's lives as academic and career development. A state-of-the-art fitness center operated on campus, a place where women who were usually covered head to toe could exercise in an all-female environment. Outside, women in black abayas and veils played badminton and kicked soccer balls. The student services director reported that she was constantly facing down groups of students who wanted to lift the campus ban on sales of junk food (candy, soda pop, sweets). And although that particular campus policy frustrated some MEWC women, one of them said that she "probably would not have thought about that part of my life at [another UAE university]. I like that the college thinks about it so I can ask questions like, 'Why do girls need sports?' "

At the Australian and UK residential colleges, which operated within coeducational university structures, students also enjoyed an out-of-class climate that put women at the center. They prized opportunities for leadership that they felt would not be available to them in mixed-gender settings. They were active in intramural sports competitions against the other colleges and reveled in their victories.

Because women's colleges were not the norm in these countries, students sometimes faced accusations that they must all be "feminists, or lesbians, or man-haters," said one woman in a UK focus group. "We have feminists and lesbians in college, of course, but I don't know any man-haters! . . . [Those myths] are just what you have to deal with when it's all girls. But it's worth it." Asked to elaborate on what was "worth it," another student responded:

> You know, we get to—we have to—do the leadership positions and college governance. And we don't have the problem with boys doing lewd things in our residences, the way they sometimes do in other colleges to annoy the girls. Or just when they've had a few too many pints [to drink]. So, we don't have that.

They did sometimes have to deal with issues of sexual harassment and assault, typically when a male outsider was alleged to have harmed a woman in the college. As I described at the opening of this chapter, the rape of an AWC student the year prior to my visit and the more recent incident with the pro-rape Facebook page were still very raw. Issues of male privilege combined with analyses of economic privilege (the men's college was known for its elite student body, which had produced more than one Australian prime minister and justice of the high court) to form the basis of robust protests from AWC students regarding the climate they faced in campus social life. On the whole, however, the climate in college was supportive and welcoming for women.

Women who were members of underrepresented racial, ethnic, religious, social class, or caste groups did not always share the same sense of warm climate with majority-group women. In India, affirmative action policies reserved spaces in higher education institutions for students from "scheduled castes," "scheduled tribes," and "other backward castes/classes" (Ministry of Human Resource Development, 2006). As in other countries (e.g., Brazil, Malaysia, the United States), the issue of "reservation," which the Indian constitution specifies, is highly fraught. And as in other countries, students who are believed by others to have been admitted under the system of reservation or affirmative action on the basis of race, ethnicity, tribe, caste, or class can face the same kind of hostile climate described earlier for women who were thought to have "taken the place of a better qualified man."

No student whom I interviewed reported any specific acts of harassment or outright discrimination, but Indian women from scheduled tribes, Australian Aboriginals, women of color in the United Kingdom, and religious minority (i.e., non-Catholic) women in the Canadian and Italian colleges spoke about a range of ways that the histories and priorities of their colleges did not reflect who these students were. Some seemed proud to be able to educate fellow students from majority groups. Comments included, "I'm probably the first Jewish person some of them have met," and "I planned an evening program to share some of my traditions." But others expressed frustration at "always being the one to say, 'No, I can't eat that' or 'No, I can't do that' because of my religion," and "It's like the woman part of me is accepted, but the Dalit part they would rather I keep to myself." Just as women's movements around the world have struggled with internal diversity, the climates at women's colleges and universities do not yet fully embrace diversity within the community.

Yuval-Davis (2011) argued in favor of using intersectional analyses to understand women's experiences, considering both intercategorical (e.g., race, class, and gender) and intracategorical (e.g., race and class within gender) approaches. Her analytic approach informs the findings of my study. Outside the women's institutions, gender, ethnicity, religion, and social class converged to influence students' chances of receiving an education, but inside the institutions, ethnic, religious, and social class diversity among women created opportunities and barriers to education.

Campus Climate for Faculty and Leaders

Although not as significant as the campus climate for students, the women's colleges and universities fulfilled a role in providing a more welcoming, supportive climate for female faculty and campus leaders than that found (or expected to be found) at coeducational institutions. Bearing in mind that the vast majority of coeducational institutions were at one time exclusively or predominantly for men, and that historically the majority of faculty and institutional leaders around the world have been men, it is no surprise that institutions designed to educate women offer a comparatively warm climate for women faculty and leaders. Even without a sample of faculty from coeducational campuses for direct comparison, evidence from my study supports this claim.

The majority of research on campus climate related to gender focuses on classroom climate (Allan & Madden, 2006), but there is also an informative literature on campus climate for faculty women, especially those working in STEM disciplines in the United States (e.g., National Academies, 2008; Sandler, 1986; Somers et al., 1998). Hart and Fellabaum (2008) analyzed 118 campus climate reports on all topics from public and private US research universities from 1991 to 2004. Of those, 112 included gender as a focus (fifty-eight included race/ethnicity, twenty-one included sexual orientation, and other categories—e.g., disability, religion, age, or social class/socioeconomic status—occurred in three to eight each); about a quarter include *only* gender as a focus. Studies of campus climate that included *only* students were less than 10% of the total, with over 90% of the studies including faculty and about a quarter including staff as well. Suffice to say, studies of campus gender climate for faculty are not rare.

Campus Climate for Faculty

What do campus-based climate studies and larger empirical studies of the gender climate for faculty and staff (i.e., administrators, department chairs, executive leaders) say? First, women remain underrepresented as faculty and leaders in most institutions in every region. The exception occurs at community, technical vocational, and teachers' colleges; at some of these less prestigious institutions, women have achieved parity in instructor roles, though in few nations do they reach 50% representation among institutional leaders (see Healy, Özbilgin, & Aliefendiğlu, 2005; Teichler, Arimoto, & Cummings, 2013; Tjomsland, 2009; West & Curtis, 2006). As with students, faculty are not distributed proportionally by gender; women are overrepresented (relative to their overall proportion of the faculty population) in humanities, social sciences, education, and nursing and underrepresented in STEM fields, business, law, and medicine.

While numbers certainly help describe the *situation* of women on the faculty, they do not provide information on the *climate* women face in the academic workplace. Unsurprisingly, the climate for female faculty at coeducational institutions resembles that for female students: they experience some instances of egregious harassment and discrimination, but more often they encounter microaggressions and lack of gender privilege that male colleagues enjoy (Findlow, 2013; Healy et al., 2005; Marschke, Laursen, Nielsen, & Rankin, 2007; Morley, 2006a). Women in STEM face particular hurdles, exacerbated by their relative rarity among these faculties (see Carrigan, Quinn, & Riskin, 2011; Donovan, Hodgson, Scanlon & Whitelegg, 2005; Gwalani, 2013; Maranto & Griffin, 2011; Yang, 2008). The discipline, institutional type and prestige, geographic region, and larger social and cultural values all shape the climate a specific faculty member encounters.

Faculty members in China, Japan, and Korea provided an example of the intersecting influences of these factors on the climate for women. The traditions in these countries of hiring graduates of one's own PhD programs, being loyal within networks of colleagues and mentors, and persistently believing in men's role as breadwinners (in spite of the fact that in these three countries it is increasingly difficult for a family to live on just one salary) have meant that generations of men find employment as STEM faculty, with fewer opportunities for women. The "old boys' network" operates with gusto to reduce the size of the academic job market for women. Women's colleges and universities in these nations provided an alternative by having doctoral programs that were open to women only. Following the tradition of hiring one's own led to a small but relevant sector of the job market in which only women were competing. One South Korean professor laughed and said, "I've never been at any other university! Maybe that is not a good thing for KWU. But for me it is very good!" The "old girls' network" operated slightly differently for a Japanese professor:

> I did my undergraduate and master's degrees here at Suburban College. After my
> PhD at [prestigious national university] I was not able to get a job there, but they were
> happy to hire me here and it has been a good place to be a professor.

The principle was the same in terms of using alumnae networks as sources of talented faculty. Both students and faculty told me that without the women's institutions, female faculty would have had fewer opportunities in STEM fields that have been dominated by men. Women faculty role models formed their own networks to hire graduates of the PhD programs of the women's universities, creating something of a self-sustaining job market for women's university alumnae.

Other features of the climate that faculty described as being positive included freedom to conduct research on gender without fear of negative reactions, lack of sexual harassment from colleagues or supervisors, and lack of inappropriate behavior from male students (particularly a factor for younger faculty). A faculty member who taught courses at another (coeducational) university in Kenya expressed relief that at KIST she was not subject to "rude looks and remarks" from male students. A UK faculty member described the freedom she felt in tutoring sessions with students, "Because we don't have to get past that whole 'Yes, you're in charge, but you're a woman so I don't have to listen to you' thing that some of the boys put up." A Japanese social science faculty member leading a research institute on gender and women's studies said that at a coeducational university she probably would not have taken on the institute because

> At a mixed university it would be hard to say our relevance. And I do not want to spend my time always saying our relevance. I want to do good research that is valued. I think it is valued here because of our history [as a women's university].

A Chinese professor said,

> When I was pregnant I did not worry about telling my department chair. I have heard in other universities that a woman will wait to tell, so that she will have more time as professor before also she is seen as a mother . . . It is good to be a mother, but once you are one, people see you differently as a professor. They maybe think that you should do more at home and less at work.

Women's colleges and universities provide a welcoming climate for female faculty, though they still operate in larger social contexts that constrain women's careers. In all of the nations in the study—as well as in the United States—gender equity in the workforce and in work-family balance remains elusive. Sexism and discrimination no doubt exist in women's institutions and in the lives of faculty who work at them. Yet the general sense from faculty was that they believed these colleges and universities provided a warm—or at least neutral—climate for academic women.

Campus Climate for Leaders

When I began a pilot study for this project, I anticipated that the leaders of women's colleges and universities might feel beleaguered or viewed as "lesser" leaders because of the lower status of their institutions vis-à-vis the dominant coeducational postsecondary paradigm in most countries. My first few interviews, conducted at the 2008 Women's Education Worldwide meeting of presidents, disproved this assumption. I went into the present study with a more open mind. In considering the overall question of the role of women's colleges and universities in the twenty-first century, I learned that one role they play is in providing a campus climate in which women thrive as executive leaders (rectors, presidents, vice chancellors, principals) and senior administrators (provosts, deans, vice presidents, vice rectors). Leading elite women's colleges in the United States has become a training ground for presidents of prestigious coeducational research universities (e.g., Nannerl Keohane went from the presidency of Wellesley College to Duke University; Ruth Simmons from Smith College to Brown University).

It is true that presidencies of women's institutions are challenging in places such as Australia, Canada, Italy, Japan, Kenya, South Korea, the United States, and the United Kingdom, in which coeducation is the norm and competition is stiff for resources and for faculty and student talent (see Altbach, 2004; Biemiller, 2011; Jaschik, 2008; Lewin, 2008; Thomas, 2008). But presidents at any type of institution face challenges as national policies seek to increase access, manage costs, and align curriculum with societal and workforce needs in an increasingly global talent market. Leaders of women's colleges and universities sit at a critical nexus in which they perform internal work in a context dedicated to women's education and external work in a context that may be less concerned with gender equity. They operate simultaneously in two climates that may not always be in alignment.

In terms of the climate on campus, presidents and senior leaders described their work in both contexts. Of the thirteen campuses I studied, women headed twelve. At the institution that was the exception (MEWC), a number of women served in senior leadership positions. Because their numbers are smaller than those for students and faculty, my data are thinner regarding the role of women's institutions in providing a supportive climate for leaders. Yet I found evidence that executives and senior faculty at some of these institutions experienced a warm climate in which to lead. In Australia, a college leader said, "Within college I feel supported by faculty and students. And with the principals of the other women's colleges here at the university and at other universities there is a camaraderie. We're women in it together."

The "hire your own" ethos I described among faculty also permeated to senior levels; several executive leaders were alumnae of the institutions they now head. "There are things I understand because I was a student and professor here," said a president in Japan. "People do not question my motivation because they know that in my heart this university is at the center." The president credited this goodwill for the political capital to make necessary, but unpopular, changes at the institution.

A few leaders came from coeducational settings and experienced the climate first as outsiders. "Such a stunning difference, to be greeted so warmly *because* I am a woman, not *in spite of* being a woman," remarked the UK college president. "The university overall does not feel like this. Women are still 'add ons' in the other [colleges]." In Canada, the principal expressed a desire to honor the college's founding Ursuline Sisters, saying,

> *I've never been in an all-women setting, so it's new to me. It has some challenges, but knowing that my judgment and motives won't be questioned on the basis of my being female—they may be questioned for other reasons!—makes me want to work harder in upholding the traditions of the Sisters.*

Goodwill and a nonjudgmental work environment may not be universal or unique to women's college presidencies. But women who lead women's colleges may receive a particular boost, as Jill Ker Conway (2001) did at her first Smith College Convocation, "when 2,000 Smith women began chanting, 'Jill! Jill!' and drumming on the floor to accentuate the shout" (p. 58). The sense of pride and ownership that Conway described Smith students as having in their institution and its female president seems to have some salutary effect on the climate for leading women's institutions. In ways that are small in the big picture of all post-secondary institutions in the world but substantial for the women who are able to move into senior roles, women's colleges and universities can provide a supportive climate in which to exercise their leadership talent.

Summary

Although women now have access to most of the world's colleges and universities and although they have reached parity with or are a majority of students in many nations, they still cannot assume that they will enjoy full equity on campus. Women's colleges and universities play a role in providing postsecondary environments in which students do not experience a chilly climate, where faculty take them seriously, and where they are guaranteed not to be a minority in STEM and other male-dominated disciplines. Spending three or four years in such an environment provides an opportunity to focus on learning and personal development without the discouragement and distractions of a chilly climate. Absent the need to lift "a ton of feathers" (Caplan, 1994), students can concentrate on lifting their sights and expectations.

Faculty and leaders at women's colleges and universities may also be out from under at least some of the ton of feathers. It is no surprise that the gender ratio of men to women among faculty and leaders is much closer at women's institutions than in higher education as a whole (Charles & Grusky, 2004; Healy et al., 2005; West & Curtis, 2006). This phenomenon is especially true in STEM fields. Women's colleges and universities play a role in providing a sector in the job market that is favorable to, if not exclusively for, female academics. Once they arrive to campus, they may find professional climates that are warmer than they would experience in predominantly male workplaces.

The question is open as to how much of this warm climate is attributable to the nature of women's colleges and universities and how much is attributable to other factors (e.g., institutional size and curriculum), as my study did not use a comparison to coeducational institutions. Evidence from around the world, however, supports the idea that one role that women's colleges and universities play in the twenty-first century is in providing not only access to higher education but also access that is free of a chilly climate and at best highly supportive of women students, faculty, and leaders.

CHAPTER FIVE

Developing Student Leaders

Women Who Will Change the World

I emerged from rush hour on the Seoul subway into a clear morning and made my way a few blocks past fashionable boutiques and coffee shops to the campus of Korean Women's University. The KWU campus sits with its main entrance at the bottom of a hill, with buildings, roads, and walking paths arrayed up the hillside. Lawns, gardens, and trees provided contrast to the hectic urban scene left behind at the campus gate. It was my fourth day on campus, and I had grown familiar with the rhythm of KWU, which like many campuses alternates between relative quiet while most students and faculty are in classes and orderly thronging during class-passing time.

But this day I noticed something different: pairs, trios, and small groups of well-dressed older women walking around. They stopped, looked at some building or sculpture or posting, and then continued on until stopping again at another point of interest. Although there seemed to be some age range across the groups, within clusters there seemed to be little. Closer observation revealed that each woman was wearing a name badge—not in and of itself unusual, as most students and staff wore identification on lanyards around their necks, but these were not ID badges. To me it looked like reunion days at Mount Holyoke, when alumnae return to campus, look at what has changed, remember what is the same, and enjoy one another's fellowship. An inquiry at the campus bookstore confirmed my impression: it was the annual meeting of the KWU Alumnae Association, which coincided with the anniversary of the university's founding in 1886. A few more inquiries and directions to the campus headquarters of the Alumnae Association yielded an invitation to observe some of the day's activities, including speeches, commemorations, and panels of prominent alumnae.

A panel on women in leadership featured three alumnae who had risen to the highest levels of their fields: a corporate CEO, the leader of a nongovernmental organization (NGO), and a distinguished research scientist. With translation help from Su-bin, a student government leader whom I had met earlier in the week, I followed the panel's discussion of obstacles and triumphs in the highly gendered worlds of Korean business, global NGOs, and science. The alumnae spoke of the power they found in relationships with other women and the need to see other women as support, not competition for the single "woman spot." They argued that leadership is not a zero-sum game that only one woman can win.

After the panel, I asked Su-bin what she thought about the messages the alumnae delivered. She replied,

> It is difficult to say, because I am leading in KWU, where gender is not the issue as
> it is when I graduate and go to work. I do not have to deal with the same gender prob-
> lems when all of us are women. So this is both good and bad. It is good because I have
> the opportunities to be elected to student government, which is not as common for
> women at other [coeducational] universities. It is bad because I am not learning how
> to lead men.

I asked if she thought she would have run for a seat in student government at a coeducational university, and she said, "I do not know. Maybe yes, I would feel confidence and know that I could do it. I am not afraid to run against a man. But at KWU that is not a factor to think about."

Su-bin told me more about her experience as a student leader. She got involved when a friend from high school, a year older, asked her to join the planning committee for a major campus event. Su-bin enjoyed having friendships with students across academic majors and class years, as well as interacting with the university administration. She took pride in student democratic self-governance: "We are for all students, and they have their voice in decisions through representation in the Student Government Association [SGA]." She described the training for SGA leaders and mentioned the student services staff who advised their organization, other student clubs, and student-led events.

I asked Su-bin how SGA responsibilities related to her major in economics. She said,

> There is no direct [relation], really. I do not even work with the finances part of the
> SGA. But I have learned to get a group moving in one direction, which is not always
> easy with KWU students—they all have an idea about the "best" way to do some-
> thing! I think that knowing how to get a group moving in one direction will be very
> useful in my work. It is like [the CEO on the panel] said, at KWU you learn how to
> lead smart women with strong ideas, and after that, leading men might seem easy!

A third significant role that women's colleges and universities play in the twenty-first century is developing students as leaders. Students on all the campuses in the study noted the ways that they had access to leadership development through student government, student publications, sport, public service, and other organizations (social, political, common interest, and so forth). In a study I conducted at a 2008 student leaders conference sponsored through Women's Education Worldwide, I found that in regions where coeducation is the norm, students often chose women's colleges and universities because they believed that they would have greater access to student leadership than at mixed-gender institutions (Renn & Lytle, 2010). And when they get to campus, they are not disappointed. Students and faculty at every institution I studied talked about the ways that without men on campus women stepped in to get things done, even if those things were not traditional for their gender, such as public speaking, policy making, leading religious observances, or carrying heavy equipment for sporting events, theater productions, and political rallies. Through "getting things done" in a student government boardroom or an intervarsity debate tournament, students built skills, confidence, and self-efficacy as leaders.

In the United States, there is a proven connection between college student involvement in activities outside the classroom and increases in desirable outcomes such as employment satisfaction, leadership, and civic engagement (for summaries, see Pascarella & Terenzini, 2005; Renn & Reason, 2013). Student leadership itself is connected to a number of other desirable student outcomes, including civic responsibility, multicultural awareness, and personal and social values (Cress, Astin, Zimmerman-Oster, & Burkhardt, 2001). Women particularly benefit from involvement as student leaders (Kezar & Moriarty, 2000; Renn & Lytle, 2010; Romano, 1996; Sagaria, 1988; Tidball, Smith, Tidball, & Wolf-Wendel, 1999; Wolf-Wendel, 2000).

Research has shown that women's colleges in the United States are good at producing leaders (Hardwick-Day, 2008; Kinzie, Thomas, Palmer, Umbach, & Kuh, 2007; Miller-Bernal, 2000, 2011; Tidball et al., 1999; Whitt, 1994; Wolf-Wendel, 1998, 2000), with a disproportionate number of women's college alumnae holding leadership roles in business, law, education, and government (elected and appointed; see Hardwick-Day, 2008). This effect persists even after accounting for the fact that, until the 1970s, the most elite universities in the United States—which have historically produced a disproportionate number of male leaders—remained all men. Even since women have had the option to attend Harvard, Princeton, and Yale, routinely among the top producers of public leaders in the United States, women's colleges have graduated more than their share of students who ascended to significant leadership posts.

In 2008, Mount Holyoke and Smith Colleges hosted a Women's Education Worldwide student leadership conference. Conference participants came from twenty-three women's colleges and universities around the world. I surveyed students using open-ended questions and found that these students were learning skills that they believed would facilitate leadership in career and society (Renn & Lytle, 2010). Students reported learning leadership and interpersonal skills such as "respect, diplomacy, compromise, [and] conflict resolution" (p. 223). They also gained confidence and self-awareness, and expressed a commitment toward serving their communities.

About two-thirds of survey respondents believed that being at a women's college in particular made a difference in their experiences as leaders. One respondent wrote, "I think as it is a women's institution, simply the probability that women become leaders, becomes higher than that of coed institution. This helps me to be a leader. In [eastern Asian nation], it is patriarchy existing in the mainstream of societies. Therefore, in coed institution, men tend to be leaders, and so the probability becomes lower. This means I have less opportunity in coed institution, I think" (Renn & Lytle, 2010, p. 225). Students believed that working against gender role expectations was easier in an all-women environment. They also reported that their institutions provided more support for their leadership development than they might get at a coeducational institution. One student believed that being in a single-sex environment "greatly impacted the richness, intensity, and focus of leadership experiences because there are more opportunities, more support and a community focus, as well as an environment conducive to my growth as a woman and in the spirit of that identity" (Renn & Lytle, 2010, p. 226). It is too soon to know whether these women will go on to become leaders in society, and currently there is no way to compare their success to that of women who attended coeducational institutions in their home nations. But they had opportunities to lead and support in doing so at their women's colleges and universities.

The potential for women's institutions to develop leaders for society is clear. As Indiresan (2002) found in her analysis of Indian women's colleges that were particularly good at promoting gender empowerment, "In brief, one of the major agendas is to empower women to build their self-confidence and self-reliance so that it would lead to economic and psychological independence leading to a better self-image and identity and ultimately raise their status in society. *Thus,*

empowered women can take leadership roles in all spheres and contribute to societal development" (p. 133; emphasis added). In considering the potential to promote women's leadership development in Arab Gulf States, Metcalfe (2011) proposed that "one area that would complement existing business culture is women
only leadership education, which would aim to build knowledge about women's
global leadership achievements and build confidence for working in mixed gender environments" (p. 144). Women's colleges and universities provide exactly
this kind of program.

Although scholarship on the role of women's institutions in producing leaders outside the United States is not common, a number of notable leaders are
alumnae of women's colleges. Burmese opposition leader Aung San Suu Kyi
attended Lady Shri Ram College in India. International jazz musician Keiko
Doi and leading architect Kazuyo Sejima are alumnae of Japan Women's University. Margaret Chan, director general of the World Health Organization, went
to Brescia University College in Canada. Ewha University in South Korea is the
alma mater of a number of distinguished women, including the first female justice on the Constitutional Court of Korea (Sohn Byoung-Ok) and the first female
prime minister of South Korea (Han Myung-sook). These few examples offer
some sense of the scope of the leadership provided by women's university alumnae. What is it about women's colleges and universities that promotes leadership
development in their students? There is the necessity to step forward, of course,
but do other aspects of the environment particularly favor growth in this dimension? I argue that they do, and they form the basis for my claim that a significant
role of women's institutions lies in their ability to cultivate women as leaders.

Student Experiences of Involvement and Leadership Development

It is a fundamental fact that women will fill all student leadership roles at single-
sex institutions, shaping opportunities for involvement and leadership for every
female student. If a woman does not step up to do something, it will not get done.
More than the absence of real or perceived competition from men for leadership,
this awareness that "of course it will be a woman" permeated the conversations
I had with students on every campus I visited. As I found in an earlier study of
women's college student leaders (Renn & Lytle, 2010), students had ideas about
what extracurricular life would be like at a coeducational institutional. Survey
responses showed that "a sizable minority of students (about a third) wrote that
they thought their leadership experience would be no different at a coeducational college. The majority of respondents, however, indicated that they thought
there would be differences. Two themes dominated the latter group's replies:

(1) more leadership opportunities for women at single-sex institutions and (2) explicit support from their institutions for women's leadership" (Renn & Lytle, 2010, p. 225). In the present study, I similarly found many women who had chosen a single-sex college at least in part because of those ideas about men's dominance in student activities, governance, and media at coeducational institutions. The taken-for-granted nature of women's involvement and leadership at the women's colleges and universities was striking. I hesitate to draw cross-national conclusions about universalized experiences of gender, but I observed the involvement and leadership development phenomenon everywhere I went.

Student Government

Student government (also called students' union, council, parliament, or house council) varies from region to region and institution to institution, but no matter what form or name it takes, student-run governance provides opportunities for involvement and leadership. In the United States, the professional field of student affairs has evolved to include a focus on training and advising student government leaders (see Council for the Advancement of Standards in Higher Education, 2012). International advocates for the student affairs and services field describe institutions' responsibility for providing guidance and opportunities for student self-governance and participation in higher education governance (Ludeman, Osfield, Hidalgo, Oste, & Wang, 2009).

A number of students I interviewed or met in focus groups were active in student governance as either elected or appointed leaders with formal positions (e.g., president, vice president, chair, warden). The head of the student parliament at MEWC was clear about the role it played in her collegiate experience, saying,

> I do learn a lot in my classes, but what I have learned through Parliament is bigger. What I learn in classes actually happens in Parliament, where we have to figure out how to solve problems, represent ourselves to [the rector], get our message out to students.

Asked if she thought she could translate these skills into a cogendered future work setting, she replied, "Of course." In her mind, there was no question that what she was learning would be applicable in her postcollege life. "Being a leader here will help me be a leader in corporate as well." The president of the student government association at the South Korean university was equally adamant: "There is no question. Being president of SGA is good for my future profession." Students' union leaders at one college in India were responsible for overseeing student taxes and the budgets of other student organizations. One student said,

> I want to go into public policy, and maybe someday run for office in my state, maybe national. This experience of being in charge—of having to answer to the constituents as well as the administration of the college—has shown me that I can do it and I like doing it.

Would she have run for student office at a coeducational institution? "Maybe. But the boys run the outfit at most mixed colleges. It's theirs." Similarly in Japan, a student leader remarked that it could be difficult for women to win elections at coeducational universities, "which is bad for girls because we all have something to learn in it."

For students in women's residential colleges within coeducational universities (Australia, Canada, Italy, the United Kingdom), college leadership could be a first step. A UK alumna told me,

> I got to know the students' union through my [college government], and felt I had the experience to run for an officer position. I won the election and it was a good way to build on the college experience in the larger university. I don't know if I'd have gotten a good start in a mixed college, or if I'd have tried at all. I was rather shy when I first came up [to college].

As an Australian student put it, her choice to join an all-women's college provided "an added bonus" where she could get something extra, "more chances to get involved and take charge" than in the coeducational colleges. An active student leader, her philosophy was "to have fun with the girls, and do a little uni[versity] along the way."

Whether they were overseeing academic honor codes, managing finances and budgets, lobbying administrators for policy changes (academic, social, or otherwise), or mastering the finer points of institutional and constituent politics, the students I encountered were learning how to lead in complex organizations. It is possible that these same women would have become student leaders at coeducational institutions, and certainly there are women in leadership roles at coeducational schools in these countries, but at an individual level there is no way to assess the value added by being in an all-women context. On a broader level, by maintaining active student governance bodies populated entirely by women, these institutions were increasing the overall number of opportunities for college women to lead.

Sport, Political Activism, and Arts

In addition to leading in student governance, women's college students lead other gender-nontraditional activities such as those in sports and politics, as well as traditionally feminine student activities (also called student associations, organizations, or clubs), including those related to performing and visual arts. Exercising leadership in these gendered contexts within the larger environment of an all-women's organization provided opportunities for development and growth. In interviews and focus groups, I also heard some students talk about how leading in these activities caused them to reflect on gender roles.

Outside the United States, students, rather than institutional departments, typically organize the infrastructure for student athletics and recreation. In these contexts, sports exist only if students take up leadership. A student in Japan reported that their campus clubs included those for basketball, tennis, and volleyball, all organized by students. Australian women's college students participated in on-campus "intercol" (short for intercollege) rivalries in swimming, rowing, field hockey, softball, tennis, basketball, and more. "There's a council of students who organize the whole schedule and matches. The council is mainly boys, except for us from the all girls colleges." Women had taken up organizing their own intramural cricket matches at Urban Comprehensive University, although, according to one student who led a team, "no one ever comes to watch like they do with the boys."

The freedom to take up leadership in sport was a particular point of pride for several women. The captain of an intramural football (known as soccer in the United States) squad in South Korea said, "It is important to me to win. Being captain I can make sure that we play our best." Was she worried about how she would appear to others as a woman interested in sport? "If there were boys here, I maybe would not play. They maybe would think I was being too masculine. It is something very good about my university—girls can play without worrying about what boys think."

In China, students availed themselves of campus athletics and recreation facilities to uphold a vibrant sport schedule with nearby universities. One student was unabashed about her participation: "I am strong and fast at basketball. My parents think it is not feminine and I will not get husband." Asked to say more about gender roles and marriage prospects, she stated, "Now I do not want a husband. Now I want to study and play basketball." She said that eventually she would be looking for a husband, "Hopefully one who likes basketball also!" But what she was learning through being an athlete and being team captain—which involved the kinds of activities typical of a coach and scheduler, much different from those of US student team captains—was that "I can organize the team, have practices and games, get things started, and these are skills that I can use outside basketball to get things done."

If women leaders in sport seemed aware that their participation was not traditional for their gender, women leaders in political activism were even more conscious of the potential risks and rewards of taking leadership for social change. A student in Australia said, "I am working for progress for indigenous people . . . being a student leader at AWC is good training for politics, because I know how hard it can be to be the one voice speaking up—and how important." She went on to describe the importance of having the women's college context as a springboard, "because there's one less layer to get through—it's not men versus women, indigenous versus white."

I was in India over International Women's Day (March 8th) and had the opportunity to participate in activities organized by the leaders of the campus Women's Development Cell. They had organized a film and a speaker (a famous actress who starred in the film shown that day) as well as a rally on campus and a Take Back the Night march through the streets off campus. Not everyone at the college understood why student leaders would invest their time in raising awareness of gender issues. As one student not involved in the Women's Day events said, "because we're all girls. No one has to point out gender to us." In a separate interview, one of the student leaders addressed this point exactly,

> Just because we are all girls does not mean that we are not subject to gender restrictions on and especially off campus. You will see that girls who come by Metro are careful to dress a certain way, and when hostel girls go out, they do, too. But if we point that out, they say we're being feminists . . . I do call myself a feminist because it's important for women to lead for women's rights. If someone sees it as a bad thing, so be it.

Several hundred students attended the film and lecture, and over two hundred students joined the rally and march, which I describe in more detail in chapter 6 in relation to gender empowerment. The day after the events, the self-described feminist student leader said, "Even when it is all girls—maybe *because* it is all girls—we need to do these things." And someone has to lead the effort.

In fields already considered "feminine," student leaders did not reflect much on how they might be simultaneously (and inadvertently) reinforcing gender stereotypes while challenging the convention that women do not lead. Organizing a cultural festival in Japan involved an array of leadership and management skills (vision setting, delegation, team building, logistics, negotiating, scheduling), yet the student who did it talked more about the value of illuminating "traditional Japanese dance, music, and poetry." Similarly, the student who mounted an art exhibit in Italy focused on the opportunity to showcase the artistic talent of students and alumnae of her college. Asked if she saw herself as a leader, she said, "No. I'm an artist who had the idea to organize the exhibit. Leaders are the bosses. I'm not the boss." Yet she had organized a committee to implement her idea and several faculty and students identified her as a leader of the event.

Traditionally feminine domains also provided a way into leadership that was culturally acceptable in societies with highly circumscribed gender roles. Getting her feet wet as a leader in an arts activity led one student in the UAE to run for the student parliament: "It was after I worked on the Film Festival that [the student services coordinator] suggested I join Student Parliament . . . I would not have joined in there before the Film Festival." KIST was a small institution when I made my visit, but an embryonic form of student self-governance was developing on the "bush" (rural) campus where a few dozen students lived. "I helped with the hostel committee, and then was asked to help with other things," said a student who became the de facto "head girl" on a campus that lacked a formal leadership and governance structure. "After discussing hostel issues with [campus executive leaders], I was more comfortable to discuss other issues with them. The other girls see this and will ask me to talk to [campus leaders], too."

Even in the arts, there are elements that involve nontraditional activities for women. In India, one student described her experience as producer of a play:

> It came time to set up the lights, and the director wanted them in such-and-such places to light the stage just right. Well, those lights are heavy! Maybe 40 or 50 kilos [100–110 pounds]. We looked around and there was no one else to do it, so I said, "Come on girls, we just have to get it done." And we did . . . I have learned that you cannot always sit around waiting for a boy to do it for you. It might take more thinking about the best way to do it, but it gets done.

This student was not sitting around waiting for a boy to take charge of other aspects of her life or career. Asked if she thought that the lesson of the lighting equipment had any application in other aspects of her academic experience, she said, "Hopefully nothing that heavy! But that idea that we can do anything boys can do is always there. No one can stop us."

Support for Becoming Leaders

In gender-traditional or gender-nontraditional activities, students at women's colleges and universities had opportunities to get involved as participants and leaders. Many of them also described the explicit ways that they felt supported by their institutions to do so. A great number of coeducational institutions around the world also provide support for student leaders, but students at the schools I visited outlined some gender-specific strategies for leadership development.

One common strategy was to provide explicit training in areas in which women from a particular region might be or feel inadequately prepared, either because they lacked prior opportunities or gender role expectations inhibited them from trying. Public speaking is one example. Because women in some contexts are expected to be seen and not heard, some women's colleges and universities—such as those in Australia, Canada, India, Japan, South Korea, and the UAE—provided training and coursework in public speaking. Managing budgets was a leadership-training topic for student leaders in Australia, South Korea, and the United Kingdom. I heard about training in leadership and professional ethics in Canada, India, and Japan. Other topics covered were time management, group dynamics, and meeting and event planning.

Providing abundant role models of women leaders in institutional leadership and faculty—and drawing from alumnae and local leaders in business, politics, and the arts—was another common strategy. Female presidents of some institutions held cultlike status among students. In South Korea: "Dr. [name] is so well known, wherever you go in Seoul." In India: "Oh, Dr. [name], she is *wonderful!*" In Italy: "She was our first rector, and she is still here. She has made our college what it is. We are so thankful for her." In Canada: "She was a law professor. Now she's our principal. And she has a family. That's not easy!"

Female faculty likewise came in for their share of role modeling and (good) example setting. "For [the students] to see me as a PhD in mathematics, and to know that I graduated from this college, it may provide some encouragement for them to lead in STEM," said one Japanese professor. An Emirati professor—who bucked convention somewhat by wearing hijab but not the full-body black abaya of Emirati national dress—remarked with a smile that the students "see how I dress, they know I went [to Europe] for my PhD. They see that I speak up. They may not ever do those things. But perhaps their daughters will!"

The sense that change in the direction of gender equity was a generations-long process was evident in considering how alumnae were held up as role models for women's leadership. Websites, campus museums, institutional histories, and campus physical features (e.g., building names, plaques, statues) all made women—especially alumnae—examples in tacit or explicit exhortation for students to emulate as leaders. Institutional websites and monitored Wikipedia pages tout well-known alumnae who were "famous firsts." One extreme example of making heroines visible may be the founder's gravesite on the Suburban College campus (a phenomenon not unique to Japan; the founder of Mount Holyoke is buried in the middle of that campus). Students at SC had a constant reminder in the leadership example of a woman who dared to return home to Japan to open a women's college after many years studying abroad. Just as every Wellesley College student knows she is following the footsteps of former US Secretaries of State Madeleine Albright and Hillary Rodham Clinton, students in Australia, Canada, China, India, Japan, South Korea, and the United Kingdom could rattle off the names of well-known leaders who shared their alma mater. They named journalists, scientists, heads of multinational corporations, politicians, high court justices, musicians, actors, and even one professional athlete. A student from Australia added with a laugh, "And of course we girls say, 'No problem! I can be like her!' Now that's a bit daunting."

Only at the Canadian women's college did one of my interviewees spontaneously raise the topic of leadership education related to diversity. Considering the call for intersectional analyses in international and global scholarship (Yuval-Davis, 2011) and issues of campus climate raised by racial, ethnic, caste, religious, or other minority women, I wondered if this area might be one that women's colleges and universities could or should add to their array of leadership development and education programs. At a minimum, students should understand that there are numerous ways to be a leader and many ways for diverse women to lead in different communities.

All of the Pieces in One Place

It seems that the "formula" these colleges and universities follow to produce generations of women leaders—and disproportionately so—involves opportunity, necessity, training, and role models, assembled in an environment that heightens awareness of gender. In the next section I discuss the purposeful nature of leadership development at these institutions. But even without intention, the supportive climate and requirements of creating their own student lives led women to take up formal and informal leadership roles. There was no one else to do it, and there was no one who could stop them. They knew they could be like the campus leaders and famous alumnae held out as examples. Expectations—of them by others and for themselves—were high. It was as the student services coordinator in China said: "All the pieces are in one place to make them leaders."

The gendered context of the women's institution seemed to make a difference for some students, such as the ones who planned the International Women's Day festivities. Similarly, a survey respondent in the Renn and Lytle (2010) study wrote, "Being a woman student leader at a women institution involves a deeper understanding of women related issues and concerns as opposed to more generalized concerning facing coed institutions. Had I been a student leader at a coed institution, certain issues such as focus on women's education, emancipation, and development, although important would have been redefined due to mixed concerns of student population" (p. 226). Not all of the students I interviewed in the thirteen institutions shared this sense of understanding gender, but some did. I asked students whether and how their experiences would be different at a coeducational college or university, and although a handful said it would not differ, a majority described ways that their opportunities would be limited. The limitation might be self-imposed—"I might not put myself up for office"—or imposed by cultural norms—"In our country, women who speak up are seen as undesirable." Other students described how the focus of their leadership might be different. The leader of a debate society said,

> *If I were at a mixed school, I think I would concentrate my energy on women's issues to make sure that women were safe on campus . . . Being at a girls' college means that I don't have to concentrate there. We are already safe.*

Even if the gendered nature of these leadership opportunities was not always on the minds of students, institutional leaders and faculty certainly understood the particular opportunity and obligation of cultivating women as leaders in all realms, no matter how explicit the connection to gender.

Institutional Goals for Leadership Development

Leadership development is an explicit mission of women's colleges and universities in all regions. Renn and Lytle (2010) found evidence of leadership as a persistent theme in the cocurriculum of women's institutions around the world. In this study, I also found evidence that faculty and administrators encourage women to participate in student governance, honor boards, entrepreneurial activities, sport, internships, academic societies, and the arts. Student participation may also be encouraged at coeducational institutions, and women may be encouraged to participate there as well. But I observed that student leadership development was an explicit agenda at these institutions, regardless of region, size, or curriculum (e.g., STEM, humanities, education, or business).

In some cases, this focus on leadership development seemed to be part of a "branding" strategy designed to attract talented students who might have other options in higher education. In areas where coeducation was the norm, and where women had abundant free choice to attend coeducational schools, women's institutions touted leadership development as an added value of attendance. Institutional taglines or marketing slogans included: *Choose to Lead, Ready to Lead; Resist the Easy Road and Become a Leader;* and *Practicing the Future.* Putting the challenge directly to students, one university urged students, *Don't Just Play the Game, Change It.* Elsewhere students were told to be *Women Who Will Change the World.* The first line in one institutional mission is "To empower women to assume leadership." In the United States, the Women's College Coalition (n.d.) advocates for attending its member colleges, where leadership development and opportunities are a selling point for this somewhat beleaguered sector of higher education. In short, women's colleges and universities do not hide this light under a bushel. They are unabashed in their promotion of leadership development for students. It is central to their mission and operation.

Women's colleges and universities backed up these bold statements about leadership in a variety of ways. The Korean university sponsored a leadership development institute, including opportunities for students and alumnae. The goal of the institute is "to develop and strengthen comprehensive and balanced leadership skills and styles for current and future women leaders." Canadian students had the option to take formal coursework through an academic program in leadership and undertake a range of cocurricular leadership development activities, including public speaking contests (first prize was a full one-year scholarship to the college) and mentoring younger women and girls in leadership.

Women's Federation University has a somewhat unique history of developing women as leaders. Founded to educate members of the All-China Women's Federation of the Communist Party of China, WFU has historically focused on preparing leaders in the area of gender equality and development. Its explicit mission is to undertake women's leadership research, and the institution sponsors a journal that disseminates research on gender and leadership, among other topics. The faculty I met were involved in some of these projects.

MEWC undertook a robust approach to developing leadership skills in young Emirati women. The curriculum and cocurriculum, as partly described in chapter 4, were designed to build confidence and skills in students who likely had few opportunities before college or outside the gates to practice leadership. The rector noted,

> *It's important for [students] to see what the world has for them, and then to see how they can fit into it within the constraints of home and family expectations. We take them on international study tours, to see cultural sites as well as business and industry. For most of our students, that's something they would not do outside of the college . . . And we bring them together with women student leaders from around the world, to get a better sense of themselves as leaders in the Emirates and in the world. How are they different from students in other countries? How are they the same? They learn from one another. That's what we do.*

MEWC regularly sponsored student leaders to attend, with appropriate staff or faculty chaperones, student leadership events outside the UAE, and particularly the women's leadership conferences sponsored through Women's Education Worldwide. MEWC also sponsored an annual weeklong women student leaders conference that brought fifty to sixty students from around the world and paired them with MEWC students. Students learned from and with one another through workshops, discussions, and notable keynote speakers. The rector viewed this activity as critical to "bringing the world to us . . . [this city] is very global, but not always in ways that our students get to interact with. We create a way for them to do that."

One Japanese university offered a "highly specialized education to develop women leaders" and hosted a national award-winning leadership education and research center under its gender equity office. The center sponsored a multilevel leadership development program for students from all academic fields. According to a faculty member who worked with the leadership development program,

> *We follow the tradition of our founding, with the idea that our students should "make a difference" through the principles of respect for others, intelligence, and confidence. We focus on three aspects: Communication through presence, discussion, and presentation. Creativity though planning, imagination, and critical thinking. Organization through teamwork, collaboration, and facilitation.*

To teach these aspects, the center operates programs in a pyramid structure, with entry-level involvement (e.g., attending events) on a wide base, opportunities that demand more skill and knowledge (e.g., chairing an event planning committee) in the middle, and the most demanding—and least common—opportunities that require the most skill (e.g., head of the student government) at the top. The program was well publicized to students. One student said, "There are some girls who do not do some part of it, but most people I know [are] doing something in the program."

In spite of the overall positive response to institutional efforts in this area, I heard from a few students that goals for leadership development and publicity about women leaders grew tiresome and, at times, overbearing. A woman in a focus group of students at one of the elite Indian colleges broke the silence on this issue:

> The college is always telling us to be this and do that. They put all of these brilliant graduates in front of us. It's intimidating. [Name] was not the CEO of a bank when she was a student. And [name] was not on the High Court when she was here. I do not see how to get from here to there.

Another student in the group focused more on the present, saying, "I am proud to be at [this college], but they push feminism and leadership too much some times. I am here because my parents wanted me here, not to become a feminist or a leader." Other students nodded their heads in apparent agreement. After taking into account the possibility of the influence of the group on individuals, I was still struck by the directness of the two women who had spoken out against the all-leadership-all-the-time messages they felt the college was sending.

More concerning than students speaking out against institutional messages were stories I heard from students about pressure they felt to excel, to be extraordinary. Women from less wealthy or less cosmopolitan families found themselves outsiders to the hearty culture of "effortless perfection" (Keohane, 2003) that they felt institutions were attempting to create through leadership development programs.[1] A first-generation student from a rural Canadian family felt

> surprised by the level of expectation . . . I decided to live in college because I thought it would provide a smaller environment, but it's a small environment with big goals for students who will go out to change the world. I wasn't really ready for that. I struggled to find my way first year.

An ethnic minority student in Australia said, "It's hard sometimes to be the only [person of color] in the room. And then to think I'm expected to become [Prime Minister]? I'm just trying to get through the semester." An Emirati woman felt "pushed" to go beyond her comfort level, causing her to withdraw from being

---

1. Derived from a study of campus climate at Duke University (United States), the term *effortless perfection* describes an expectation that women can and should do everything, do it well, and make it look easy. Women should be beautiful, smart, and accomplished without breaking a sweat. See Keohane (2003) for the Duke report.

involved in student organizations. Institutions' messages about and support for leadership development occasionally had these unintended consequences. For the most part, however, institutional efforts toward student leadership development seemed to have a beneficial, or a least neutral, impact on students.

Summary

Women's colleges and universities fulfill a role in preparing students to become leaders on campus and in society. In regions where coeducation is a common (or the most common) context for women students in higher education, these institutions do so with disproportionate success, sending more than their expected share of women into leadership roles in business, government, education, medicine, and law. One reason for their success is obvious: there are no men to compete for leadership positions on campus, so women must and do lead in a range of student organizations. At a more nuanced level, students also felt free from men's view. They could take up sport or governance or anything else without worrying about how their male peers would perceive them. A student attending a women's college or university was free, at least on campus, from worrying (as one student's mother did) that if she played sports she would never find a husband. The women's colleges and universities created a bracketed world, inside and outside the classroom, in which students could participate for three or four years without some of the relentlessly gendered expectations beyond the campus gates. And students had the "excuse"—if they needed one—that they had to get involved because there were no men to do the work instead. A woman could explain herself to skeptical outsiders (parents, boyfriends, siblings, potential employers) as having taken on a "masculine" task because *someone* had to, and that someone would always be a woman at her college or university.

The lessons learned through these activities could be carried out into the world—at least that was the expectation of the institutions as they attempted to mold women who would change the world, choose to lead, and resist the easy road. Owing to significant success in graduating future leaders, faculty and leaders at these colleges and universities had reason to be optimistic. The well-defined, purposeful leadership development programs on some campuses took this optimism a step further by institutionalizing the commitment to student leadership. Looking ahead in the twenty-first century, when gender equity seems possible but is not inevitable, women's colleges and universities may have a particular role to play in developing women to be local, national, and global leaders.

CHAPTER SIX

Gender Empowerment for Campus and Community

On March 8, 2011, I was in Delhi visiting Elite College. It was International Women's Day. The morning papers featured glamorous advertisements for perfume, jewelry, and other posh gifts to make the women in one's life feel special on their day. The concept of commercializing femininity stood in contrast to my understanding of Women's Day as a commemoration and recognition of movement toward women's equality, an understanding reinforced by my Facebook feed that morning, which contained quotes and links to media honoring women's struggles and triumphs. I looked forward to the day ahead, which included my usual rounds of interviews and focus group meetings, plus the Women's Day events on campus to which I had been invited by the student organizers.

Activities began midafternoon with a screening of the 2006 Indian drama *Dor*. The film is the story of an independent Muslim woman and a traditional Hindu woman whose lives connect when the husband of one is alleged to have murdered the husband of the other. Because the film was in Hindi, with parts in Urdu, I got simultaneous translation from a staff member, though the acting and cinematography were nearly enough to follow the story without any translation. The centrality of women's stories to the film was clear, and it seemed a good choice for a Women's Day showing.

The auditorium was packed with several hundred EC students, in part because of the promised postfilm speaker, one of the lead actresses from the movie, Gul Panag—a former Miss India, international debate champion, holder of a bachelor's degree in mathematics and master's in political science, and model for the men's magazine *Maxim*. The previous fall she had spoken out about unsafe conditions for women in Delhi following her participation in the Delhi Half Marathon, during which she was sexually harassed and groped by male runners (Sharma, 2010). She seemed to me to embody the paradox of Women's Day as an occasion to celebrate glamour and to take seriously discrimination and harassment against women. She did not disappoint on either count. Panag came down the center aisle of the auditorium carrying a large designer handbag and wearing five-inch heels, a sleeveless sheath dress that hit above the knee, and large sunglasses, which she propped on her head. When her remarks about Women's Day failed to satisfy audience members looking for a more distinctly feminist message, she sharpened her comments to clarify her stance as a proponent of women's equality.

The next activity was a rally on campus, followed by a Take Back the Night march. Students, faculty, staff, and community members sat in a circle on blankets on the grassy lawn. A local folk musician got the crowd to sing feminist organizing songs in Hindi and English. We sang and we chanted. We made signs to carry on the march in Hindi and English, reading *No Means No! Women Belong Everywhere! Our Bodies, Our Lives.* As dusk fell, we held a candlelight vigil to close the rally and begin the march.

Out through the campus gate, over two hundred students, faculty, and community members (and one visiting researcher from the United States) took to the streets with signs, candles, slogans, and chants. About a dozen police armed with machine guns accompanied us for our protection, I was told. In conversation with a student marcher, I asked more about the likelihood of violence against a group of two hundred women marching at night.

> *Ma'am, look around us. Do you see any other women out at night? No. It is not safe, certainly not for a woman alone. Even if no one hurt her, they would say bad things to her and about her.*

I watched men on the street watch us go by. They were gathered around food stands or sat in circles on the ground. We went through impoverished neighborhoods and by a few foreign embassy residences. We kept up the chants, including "Short skirts, high heels, we can wear what we feel!," in reference both to the notion that a woman is to blame if she is sexually assaulted and to the day-to-day restrictions placed on women's bodies in public spaces. I thought about the way that Gul Panag had dressed and wondered if students who couldn't feel safe to wear a sleeveless top in public (even on the hottest days) envied her for more than her glamorous lifestyle.

Press coverage of the march was generally positive and informative, noting the role of community women in the events. Two days later, the newspaper featured a story of a student from another college in Delhi; she had been sexually assaulted in public, in daylight, crossing a street near her campus, and no one intervened on her behalf. What did the EC students think of this event, occurring within twenty-four hours of their march? One said, "Our work is not done." Would she continue this kind of activism after she graduated? "I will. Until it is safe for girls and women to be out alone at night—and during the day."

Along with providing access, a warm climate, and opportunities for leadership, women's colleges and universities promote gender empowerment in society generally and among students and faculty. Whether part of a purposeful strategy for social and economic development—as in the Indian Subcontinent, the Middle East, and Southeast Asia—or emerging more organically from local needs and interests, women's higher education institutions have contributed historically and in contemporary societies to movements for gender equality and women's participation in the workforce. From their beginnings to today, these colleges and universities have provided intellectual, cultural, social, and political homes for women, women's studies, and activist movements for equal rights and gender equity.

The term *gender empowerment* has a number of definitions, some of which are strongly debated among feminist scholars, activists, and international development professionals. The United Nations Development Programme (UNDP) assesses gender empowerment at a national level using its Gender Empowerment Measure (GEM), which examines "whether women and men are able to actively participate in economic and political life and take part in decision-making" (UNDP, 1995, p. 73). The GEM has three components: (1) proportion of seats held by women in national parliaments, (2) percentage of women in economic decision-making positions, and (3) female share of all income earned. To round out the picture, the UNDP combines the GEM, which it describes as a measure of agency, with the Gender-related Development Index (GDI), which measures inequality in the dimensions of its Human Development Index (health, education, and living standards). Critics consider the GEM and GDI to be, among other things, inherently Eurocentric, overly focused on economic measures, lacking in complexity, and overbalanced in favor of the global north over the global south (see Kabeer, 2005; Klasen, 2006; Lee, 2011; Syed, 2010).

Summarizing a previous description she provided in a UNESCO report (Stromquist, 1995), Stromquist (2002) stated, "Empowerment consists of four dimensions, each equally important but none sufficient by itself to enable women to act on their own behalf. These are the cognitive (critical understanding of one's reality), the psychological (feeling of self-esteem), the political (awareness of power inequalities and the ability to organize and mobilize), and the economic (capacity to generate independent income)" (pp. 22–23). This richer definition of empowerment, when applied to the case of women, describes the sort of gender empowerment activities I observed at the women's colleges and universities I visited. These institutions were promoting women's cognitive, psychological, political, and economic development toward gender equality in their communities and beyond.

Empowering from within Women's Movements

Gender empowerment (albeit perhaps not always labeled as such) has been a role of women's institutions since their beginnings. They have contributed to women's movements around the world by providing intellectual homes for and communities of educated women (Batson, 2008; Coats, 1994; Harwarth, 1997; Horowitz, 1984, 1994; Palmieri, 1995; Seat, 2008; Solomon, 1985). To be sure, having a college degree is not a requirement for working for social change; I do not mean to undervalue the contributions of labor movements, community organizing, and other forms of women's activism. But in this analysis of the roles of women's colleges and universities, I highlight their historical and contemporary contribution to feminist and other women's movements. There are arguments about the value of gender "segregationist" or "separatist" tactics in political action, just as there are arguments about the value of single-sex or coeducational schools. In chapter 7, I describe some of the potential drawbacks or paradoxes of separate institutions for women. In considering gender empowerment, however, they appear to perform an important, if not irreplaceable, function.

A particular role they play within institutions is in hosting women's studies programs and research centers. Bird (2002) called women's studies "the academic arm of the women's liberation movement" in North America and the United Kingdom (p. 139). As an example of this phenomenon, Ganguly-Scrase (2000) noted the importance of women's universities in creating spaces for women's groups outside Indian political parties, where they previously resided. In the 1970s, "There was also a proliferation of scholarly work on women's status, the establishment of research organisations on women's studies such as the Centre for Women's Development Studies in New Delhi and the Research Center for Women's Studies, SNDT Women's University in Bombay" (Ganguly-Scrase, 2000, p. 91). The transformation of an "activist role into an academic curriculum" was an important step in the progression and contribution of women's research centers in India (Lal, 2009). In the mid-1980s in South Korea, "Women students and organizers from the labor movement of the 1970s, together with a group of professors from Ewha University (the first institution to provide formal education for women and girls in Korea), organized study groups, put together the first women's studies courses, and developed the Institute of Women's Research" (Louie, 1995, p. 420). This transformation is not without tension, as "Women's Studies Centres are caught often in an identity crisis about whether they belong to mainstream academia, or to the autonomous agenda of non-government organisations" (Lal, 2009, para. 8). Working within this tension is an ongoing challenge. In the United States it is also a challenge to see that women's studies and centers at women's colleges do not become seen as a "containment strategy" to keep progressive ideas from scaring away more conservative students (Sahlin, 2005, p. 164). Women's studies is not a field exclusive to women's colleges and universities (see Stromquist, 2001a, for discussion of women's studies worldwide), though some scholars argue that the field is essential to the survival of women's colleges (see Sahlin, 2005).

An ongoing debate about the value of segregating women students parallels the debate about segregating women's studies within programs and departments. Some advocates of "gender mainstreaming" believe that "gender tracking in 'regular' academic disciplines and in women's studies continues to be a barrier to the empowerment of women" (Jayaweera, 1997b, p. 251). Countering that university-based scholarship on women is a viable means for advancing gender empowerment, Lal (2009) claimed that "the network of Women's Studies Centres which covers this vast country through its universities can become an instrument for identifying women's issues in India which require priority attention" (para. 65). The particular role of women's institutions as intellectual centers (literal or figurative) for women's studies and other scholarship on women and gender equality is important for gender empowerment both historically and in the twenty-first century.

Another contribution of women's colleges and universities is in creating "female institutions" where women form communities without men. Historian Leila Rupp (1985) noted, "Estelle Freedman has suggested that female institutions are central in keeping the women's movement alive; her argument about the necessity of separatism rests implicitly on the importance of women's communities in women's colleges, settlement houses, unions, and women's organizations" (pp. 720–21). Rupp continued the argument, "Although feminist scholars do not agree on the relationship between women's culture and politics, it is clear that community building has played a central role in women's activism throughout American history" (p. 721). Evidence collected during my study demonstrates that the physical, intellectual, and symbolic spaces of women's higher education institutions also contributed to contemporary women's culture and politics outside the United States.

Contributions to Gender Empowerment Goals and Strategies

Just as they work from inside women's movements, women's postsecondary institutions likewise function within national and global agendas for gender equality. That is, governments, national NGOs, and international NGOs view women's education as a key to economic and social development as articulated in the UN Millennium Development Goals (Jensen, 2011) and national policy (e.g., in India, by the Ministry of Women and Child Development, 2001, as described by Chanana, 2007). For reasons described in previous chapters, single-sex institutions are in some regions the only or the most desirable format for providing this education. Women's colleges and universities thus play a role in enacting development goals related to women's empowerment.

In keeping with the direction of the UN Millennium Development Goals (see Jensen, 2011), a number of nations have placed educating girls and women at the center of development strategies for women's economic empowerment. It is widely accepted that increased education is positively linked to literacy, age at marriage, contraceptive use, economic participation, and reduced child mortality, among other indicators (Jensen, 2011; Robinson-Pant, 2004; Roudi-Fahimi & Moghadam, 2003). The UAE, for example, has actively promoted girls' and women's education (Al Qasimi, 2007), as have national policies in China, India, and Kenya, among others. I found that in the UAE and India the institutions I studied contributed to this goal by providing access. In Kenya and China, where a small minority of all female students attended women's universities, the contribution is minimal but consistent with larger development goals. There is evidence that whether it happens at single-sex or coeducational (where accessible) universities, increasing women's education does indeed increase women's ability to participate in the workforce, even if it is a gender-segregated workforce, as is common in the UAE and other Gulf States, including Bahrain, Qatar, and Saudi Arabia (Jamjoom & Kelly, 2013; Metcalfe, 2011).

Using education as a means toward economic empowerment seems sensible, but it also comes under substantial criticism as a neoliberal scheme that (at best) masks the role education plays in sustaining global systems of inequity and (at worst) perpetuates oppression and gender violence at the most basic levels of society. Robinson-Pant (2004) summarized neoliberal arguments for educating women and a parallel gender empowerment agenda that operates among global development agencies (see also Ali, 2002; Metcalfe, 2011; Stromquist, 2012; Vavrus, 2002). She criticized "simplistic definitions of 'gender empowerment' and 'cultural barriers' that inform current policy debates about women's education in the international context" because they "prevent any real attempts to understand and explore alternative values and viewpoints" (Robinson-Pant, 2004, p. 474). A paradox exists where women's colleges embrace feminist and empowerment goals for their students and communities while reproducing gender-, race-, religious-, and class-based inequalities in society. In chapter 7, in which I discuss symbolic roles that women's institutions play, I describe these critiques in more detail.

For the purposes of understanding the role of women's colleges and universities in gender empowerment, one must understand that they operate within local, national, and global systems of political and economic forces to which they are not immune (see Marginson & Rhoades, 2002). The extent to which the institutional leaders I interviewed acknowledged these forces and their impact varied, as did the leaders' attitudes toward them. Students, for the most part, were unaware of how their alma maters might fit into larger economic and human development schemes.

Contributions to Gender Empowerment

What kinds of contributions did women's colleges and universities make to gender empowerment? How did they fulfill this role? I identified four areas through which they contributed to gender empowerment: intellectual, cultural, symbolic, and activist. The categories are not discrete, as some activities overlap. My point is to convey a sense of how women's colleges and universities contributed to gender empowerment more broadly rather than to present a typology of such contributions.

Intellectual Life

In previous chapters I described some of the ways that students benefitted from a focus on intellectual development in an environment that supported their learning and growth. But several of the institutions in this study also played a role in gender empowerment in their communities by serving as intellectual homes for women and for research on women and gender. The means through which they created these intellectual and physical spaces included women's or gender studies programs, centers for research on women and gender, and a critical mass of faculty interested in bringing together women (and sometimes men) to explore intellectual and academic questions related to girls' and women's lives.

Women's Federation University (WFU) in China served as an intellectual anchor within the All-China Women's Federation (ACWF). Together with the ACWF's Women's Studies Institute of China, WFU has pioneered the field of women's studies in China. The name of WFU's Institute for Advanced Study in Gender *and Development of Women Cadres* (emphasis added) serves as a reminder of the university's close relationship with the ACWF and the Chinese Communist Party (CCP). The historic role of the university—founded in 1949 as New China Women's Vocational School, later the Women Cadres' School, the Management Institute of the All-China Women's Federation (1984), and the China Women Administrators' College (1987)—persists in its continued relationship with the ACWF even now that the university operates under the approval of the Ministry of Education.

WFU plays an explicit role in gender empowerment. It offers a four-year undergraduate degree in women's studies through a freestanding department in the School of Sociology and Law. The bachelor of arts degree in women's studies is the only one in China authorized by the national education ministry. Of the two students I met who chose WFU for reasons other than it being the only university in Beijing that their gaokao scores would qualify them to attend, both did so to be women's studies majors. One said, "I know that it is unusual for girls in China, but I knew that I wanted women's studies. I was glad to know I could do it here." Even if the women's studies major was only one of nineteen majors offered by the university, its faculty taught every student at some point, as WFU required all students to take an introductory women's studies course. About this requirement, one of the women *not* majoring in women's studies remarked,

> At the beginning I thought it was just something I had to do and that I was already a woman so what would I learn from a class about women. Then I realized that there was much I did not know about women in my country and around the world. So I took one more [women's studies] class by choice . . . The classes change how I think about my major, which is finance management. There are not as many women who work in finance. Because of the [women's studies] classes I am more ready to be with men [in the workforce]. I understand how they have advantages and I must be aware.

In addition to providing gender empowerment for individual students, WFU faculty in women's studies formed networks with other women's and gender studies scholars in the city and nation, attending conferences and sponsoring a leading Chinese journal. They thereby supported the academic and intellectual infrastructure of women's studies in China.

Outside the university, WFU participated in a number of efforts toward lifelong learning and community education, all with a gendered approach. Through the ACWF, the institution connected with a number of social and political alliances dedicated to improving girls' and women's education, especially outside the major metropolitan areas. One example was a partnership that the ACWF facilitated among WFU, community agencies, and elementary, middle, and secondary schools in another province. The goal of this partnership was to improve the level of education of women at all points in the life course and to develop women's community leadership capacity. A faculty member working with the partnership told me,

> I come from [that province]. It is very important to me that more girls and women
> have opportunity to learn and maybe go to college. Even if they do not, they will have
> better lives when they know that they are equal to their husbands.

Asked if women's studies researchers at institutes and coeducational universities were involved in similar efforts, she said, "Yes, but not the same. Here it is part of our work, what we are *meant* to do. There it might be more something extra." In Beijing and beyond, WFU played a role in gender empowerment.

Other countries lacked the same political mandate to make academic and intellectual contributions to gender empowerment, but several women's colleges and universities did so without inducement. At the Catholic College of Mumbai, I attended a book reading and release event for the ethnography *Why Loiter? Women and Risk on Mumbai Streets* (Phadke, Khan, & Ranade, 2011). Organizers planned the event in conjunction with the gender studies center on campus and featured an alumna author. Authors, alumnae, college members, community-based feminists, and gender activists attended the packed event in an artists' loft space in the city. Why didn't they hold the event on campus—the campus I described previously as a garden oasis in a former raj's palace? The director of the gender studies center explained,

> We do have many programs here [on campus], but it is also important to get off campus as well. We cannot be cloistered in the college, away from the real lives and real work of women. Of course we all live in that world, but it is so important for the college to reach outside itself.

College faculty, staff, and students do some of the legwork for these events, she noted, as a way to "use some of the privilege we have as being part of the college." The center sponsored other gender empowerment activities—including lectures by local and visiting feminist scholars, research symposia, and feminist reading groups—which are similar to those found in Indiresan's (2002) multi-institution study of "pace-setting" Indian women's colleges that promoted gen-der development initiatives.

The South Korean university was well known for research in many areas (STEM, medicine, law, social science, humanities), and esteemed for its Asian Center for Women's Studies (ACWS). ACWS is over 20 years old and hosts a lon-gitudinal international research project to promote the development of women's studies in China, India, Indonesia, Japan, Korea, Philippines, Taiwan, and Thai-land. ACWS sponsors an English-language academic journal, *Asian Journal of Women's Studies*, which is a key resource for scholars around the world seeking women's and gender studies research from and about Asia. Korean Women's University thereby supports a community of scholars working toward gender empowerment through scholarship.

National Women's University (Japan) played a similar role through its insti-tute for gender studies. The institute-sponsored international symposia themed on topics such as work-life balance from gender-sensitive perspectives, global feminisms, gender and international development, and economic affairs in the Asian/Pacific region. They published gender studies journals in English and Japanese. As a national university, they worked in partnership with the govern-ment, including the Gender Equality Bureau (a cabinet-level office); the Ministry of Foreign Affairs; and the Ministry of Education, Culture, Sports, Science, and Technology. A faculty leader in the institute noted,

> We are very glad to have the master's degree [in gender and international develop-ment] and the interdisciplinary doctoral degree [in gender studies]. When we put them together with our faculty and our international programs like the symposium we can see intellectual capacity development. We see ourselves as a source for new generations of gender studies scholars in Japan.

NWU was empowering new gender studies scholars—all of whom were women, I ascertained—with strong research training and a sense of mission to work in academe, government, or NGOs on issues of gender equity and women's rights. They were not a large center with hundreds of students, but over time, they had created a strong pipeline for gender studies scholars and a ripple effect in the field in Japan, across Asia, and in other regions where their graduates went to work.

Cultural Life

In addition to contributing to gender empowerment through intellectual activ-ities, the women's colleges and universities I studied contributed through cultural activities and outreach. Like coeducational institutions around the world, they sponsored activities that brought together community members for arts and cultural activities. But in some cases they also sponsored activities that specifically created and sustained what I call "women's culture," consciously gendered spaces in which women gather in safe environments to discuss women's and gender issues and to share emotion (joy, anger, grief) through cultural expressions such as rituals. Whether gender empowerment came about incidentally as an outcome of women attending cultural events or intentionally, as in the case of the purposeful creation of women's culture, the contributions of the women's colleges and universities are clear.

Considering one meaning of "culture" as expressed in art, music, poetry, and dance, these institutions offered several examples that illuminate their contributions to gender empowerment. At Collegio della Donna in Italy, the college took seriously its role in elevating women's participation in cultural activities. An art gallery featured works by female artists. A concert series brought together audiences interested in contemporary female composers and musicians. The rector noted, "Our country is the foundation of much Western art and culture. We take this seriously . . . At CDD we play our part by demonstrating the women's potential and accomplishments in art and music."

Both Japanese institutions took their roles seriously, too, by cultivating cultural opportunities to bring campus and community together. Both sponsored exhibitions of traditional dance, music, and poetry, sometimes performed by students, sometimes by guest artists. A focus on women in these traditions brought forward the richness and complexities of Japanese women's history. Discussions after some performances provided opportunities for interested audience members to deepen their understanding of women and gender in Japan. An administrator told me,

> *There are some older women from the city who come to the whole series [of concerts].*
> *They are very knowledgeable and talk about what they know about music history and*
> *about women in Japan. Then I think they go to dinner together and talk more. It is a*
> *chance for them to be out of their houses, away from their husbands and children . . .*
> *So they have this way to show their knowledge at the concert, and then to be together*
> *with other women.*

In this case the cultural opportunity became an occasion for a group of women from outside the university to form a community. The extent to which this community was empowering may be limited, but in a societal context that tightly constrained opportunities for older women to demonstrate expertise in public settings, the concerts provided an occasion to do so. The fact that the subject was music made it more socially acceptable for them to have a voice than had it been business or politics.

The three Indian institutions used cultural activities to bring the community to campus. Indian colleges and universities embrace the tradition of a university festival, or fest. Institutions compete with one another to hold the largest or most popular fest in their region. In India, university fests typically include intercollegiate competitions in sport; Hindi and English public speaking and writing; as well as academic exhibitions and cultural displays of music, drama, dance, film, and traditional and contemporary visual arts (see www.knowafest.com for examples and schedules of university fests across India). Colleges and universities name their fests distinctively (an institution is likely to use the same name year to year) and then theme them annually. According to students at the three institutions, attendees are students from other institutions, though some community members may come as well, particularly to the less raucous, daytime events. Fests often last two or three days, with daytime and evening activities.

The three Indian institutions I studied all placed an emphasis on women or gender in their festival name or annual theme. At Elite College in Delhi, a student said,

> We choose a theme each year that can include attention to women's issues. It might not be direct, like "women empowerment," but it might be about equality or justice. It's about having fun, too, so there are parts that have not much to do with the theme. But the speaking and writing contests often have something to do with gender. We don't do this to give our girls an advantage, but sometimes it does and we don't mind it!

Asked how students from coeducational institutions felt about being at the women's college campus, she said, "They really don't mind it. Lots of our friends go to mixed schools, so they have seen our school anyway. The boys are sometimes curious."

The opportunity to compete with men and women from other institutions (including some men's colleges) and to show off their campus and event-planning skills was a source of pride for students at all three institutions. It fit with the themes I presented in chapter 5 on leadership development. By organizing and presenting a large cultural, academic, and sporting event to an audience including their peers from other institutions, students developed a sense of gender empowerment, a spirit that "we girls can do anything." A fest organizer at the comprehensive university said with evident pride, "When my mum saw the photo [of our stage set up] in the [city newspaper], she was so surprised that girls could do all that without boys. Perhaps other people see the photo and are also surprised." In this case, contributing to cultural life became a vehicle for empowerment, as well as whatever gender empowerment might derive from the cultural elements of the fest itself.

In a different way, a women's center operating out of Canadian University College served as a cultural center for women across the city and region. The written "herstory" on the institution's website notes that four women who "envisioned a place where women could join together to explore and celebrate the sacred in their lives" founded the center in 1990. The founders recognized CUC as a woman-led institution—and now the only remaining women's college in Canada—and approached the Ursuline Sisters to request affiliation and meeting space. The center is explicitly feminist in orientation and notes on its website that it is "inspired by the feminist perspective 'the personal is political.'" Its goals include informing women about a range of issues such as women's rights, human rights, feminist spirituality, and social justice. Events include a host of activities designed to provide space for women's spirituality and culture to thrive: rituals, book readings and discussions, lectures, art shows, concerts, and workshops.

The center is not a women's or gender studies center, though scholars in these areas are frequent guests. The organizational structure is collectivist, there is a director who is a CUC employee, and students from the college provide staff support through a work-study program. The center acts beyond being a campus women's center to serve the city and region. It is in and of the college, but its history and vision have always bridged community and campus. By promoting women's culture through ritual, spirituality, arts, intellect, and activism, the center provides a foundation for gender empowerment and an entrée into a network of women's organizations in the city, region, and nation. Its role in gender empowerment through sustaining "women's culture" is clear.

Symbolic Contributions

Women's colleges and universities play roles as symbols that advance gender empowerment. Most were symbolic in their founding, as signals to the world that women's roles were changing. Many institutions act as ongoing symbols of gender empowerment as well. In chapter 7, I discuss larger issues related to the ways that women's colleges and universities play a role—sometimes a paradoxical one—through their symbolic presence. Here I discuss the specific contributions to gender empowerment.

The opening of higher education institutions for women has often been considered a symbol of changing gender roles and the potential for women's empowerment through education (Ajabaili, 2011; Altbach, 2004; Harwarth, 1997; Knight, 2004; Kodate, Kodate, & Kodate, 2010; Malik & Courtney, 2011; Miller-Bernal, 2011; Solomon, 1985; Thelin, 2011). The website of University Women's College describes it as having begun as the " 'third foundation' for women students at [its university] at a time when [the university] had the lowest proportion of women undergraduates of any university in the UK." It opened access and also sent a symbolic message that the institution must take seriously the education of women.

When the ACWF named its school for "female cadres," it sent a signal about its intended role for women in the CCP: they should be trained for leadership and taken seriously in the party. The continued existence of the university, under "the leadership of All-China Women's Federation and the guidance of the Education Ministry of China," is a contemporary symbol of women's role in the party. And the CCP periodically showcases the institution as an example of China's commitment to gender equity (see Dan & Zhu, 2012).

Urban Comprehensive University in India opened to provide vocational training and education for adult women, specifically widows. Culturally, widows in India faced dire circumstances, considered valueless without a husband and a burden on their in-laws; they were (and still are in some families) treated as servants at best, slaves at worst (for more on this phenomenon, see http://widows ofindia.de/?lang=en). UCU not only served the students who made their way to the fledgling institution in 1896, but also stood as a symbol against the abuse and mistreatment of widows in particular and women in general. Its mission remains both practically and symbolically one of gender empowerment, with an active adult education program for women and purposeful engagement with gender issues. Said one dean,

> We go back to our history, in serving poor women, to consider how to advance today.
> It would be easy to fill our university with only the top students from the best schools,
> but we want to show that women from all backgrounds can learn and be successful.
> Our nonformal programs are especially good for this.

The university has dozens of constituent colleges and schools, each with some symbolic role to contribute to gender empowerment. The stated mission of the law school, for example, is "for the empowerment of women and to impart legal education to girls." Despite its size (70,000 students), as a nonelite university UCU is not as well known as the two Indian colleges I visited. Yet it stands as a symbol in the community for gender empowerment through education and inclusion of adult women.

In Kenya, where all other higher education institutions are coeducational, KIST offers symbolic support for gender empowerment in STEM fields. Offering only these areas of study, there is no question about its purpose or how it expects to empower women. "Our main objective is to bridge the gap in gender representation in higher education," states the chancellor on the institutional webpage. His statement continues:

> We belong to . . . a sisterhood [of universities] that is committed to improving the lives of women by empowering them through scientific and technological education and training . . . Women have continued to make strides toward empowerment. More power to one ultimately means more power to all. Interventions in the development field have shown that men support women's empowerment when it enables women to bring the much-needed resources into the family or community or when it challenges power structures that have oppressed and exploited the poor of both sexes. We can only empower women by educating and training them. This is where our work at [KIST] begins.

KIST operates as an instrument and symbol of gender empowerment; given its small size when I visited, its larger impact at the time may have been more symbolic than instrumental.

From their foundings to their contemporary existence, women's colleges and universities have acted as symbols that support gender empowerment for their students and alumnae, but also beyond the campus gates in public discourse about women's roles. It is uncommon in most places in the twenty-first century to see pitched ideological debates about girls' and women's education play out in media or political arenas as they did a hundred years ago or even in the late twentieth century (for examples of the debates in different regions, see Bailey, 2001, on China; Bruneau, 1992, on late imperial China and early modern Europe; Chege & Sifuna, 2006, on Kenya; Karlekar, 1986, on Bengal; Rose, 1992, on Japan; Solomon, 1985, on the United States; and Spender, 1987, on Britain). In these debates, women's colleges were often lightning rods for opponents and beacons of hope for proponents of women's education.

As is clear from present-day terrorist attacks on girls and women pursuing education in Pakistan and Afghanistan, however, resistance reaches lethal levels in some regions where single-sex schools, colleges, and universities have become symbols—to some people—of unwelcome change in society. As appalling as the attacks are, they demonstrate the power of women's institutions as symbols, for if girls' and women's education was considered unimportant or nonthreatening, it would not require such a severe response. In their horror, these attacks show the depth of fear raised by women's colleges' and universities' potential to contribute to gender empowerment locally, nationally, and in the public consciousness.

Activism

If the first three areas in which women's colleges and universities contribute to gender empowerment seem a bit abstract, contributions made through activism—by students and faculty, often in collaboration with community members—are more concrete. Activism means different things in different cultures. Just the idea of women leaving home to attend university is a highly activist concept in some places (e.g., in parts of India, Kenya, Pakistan). In other communities, activism might involve organizing people around causes and taking up pickets. In both cases, and many in between, women's colleges and universities play a role in gender empowerment.

The International Women's Day scenario I described at the start of this chapter is a good example of public organizing. EC students and faculty brought together campus and community activists for events within and outside the college gates. City papers covered the events, extending awareness of the rally and march beyond those neighbors who saw and heard us go by.

Activism generated from within the women's center at the Canadian college also took on a public face, including that city's Take Back the Night march. The center assumed a particular role in organizing remembrance and activist responses to the massacre of fourteen women students in the School of Engineering at Montréal's École Polytechnique in 1989 by a young man who believed his admission to the school was threatened by women's admission. The annual commemoration is a ritual and an activist event open to the community, held on the women's college campus. The center provides a gathering space for campus and community activists. Its mission includes being "part of the vibrant women's network on campus and in the [urban] area. It links with and supports other women's groups in the community who work to dismantle unjust structures and to embody life-giving relationship with all that is created." While this statement might sound to some people like a gentle or intellectual sort of activism, a faculty member assured me that women who connected through the center were "perfectly capable of causing a ruckus when necessary. The Ursulines were Sisters, true, but they were activists in education and social justice. It's our tradition."

Other campuses featured activist roles in gender empowerment, in part through graduating women who became prominent leaders in gender equity and feminist activism. Around the world, I observed the sort of "gender sensitization" that Indiresan (2002) found in her study of Indian women's colleges: among the Chinese students who went to WFU only because it was in Beijing but then took a required women's studies course and awakened to gender awareness; among the vocational business students at MEWC who learned that they could (and perhaps should) raise their voices; among the Australian students outraged at the privilege enjoyed by students in the men's college across the fence; and among Japanese and Korean students who began to ask why their female faculty in STEM were not hired at coeducational national universities. The combination of gender awareness and obtaining a higher education primed alumnae to contribute as activists inside and outside systems of power. An Italian alumna told me, "As a woman in business, I do not make myself stand out as a *femminista*. But I always look for ways to make the company more friendly for women to work." A faculty member in India pointed to a newspaper clipping about an alumna pinned to a board.

She works to try to make a dent in the child marriage situation in the rural area she came from . . . Here she was involved in political actions about marriage, now she works directly in villages to educate mothers about the advantages of waiting until the daughters are at least through primary school, even better through secondary.

There is evidence that female students in coeducational institutions may fail to see gender inequities in higher education (see Morrison, Bourke, & Kelley, 2005; Webber, 2005), and certainly not all students in women's colleges and universities undergo a gender awareness transformation. But many do, and carry this transformed self into the world and into activism on behalf of gender equity.

Summary

The historic mission of women's colleges and universities supports their ongoing role in cultivating gender empowerment on campus and in their local communities. Whether from an intrinsic, mission-driven impulse or as part of a larger strategy for empowerment and development, these institutions make a number of intellectual, cultural, symbolic, and activist contributions to women's movements. Not all of the colleges and universities I studied made all types of contributions, but they each made some.

If there were no women's colleges, could gender empowerment still happen? Most likely, yes. But some of the contributions that these institutions were making to gender empowerment would be difficult to replicate at coeducational universities or from community-based organizations. Specifically, the notion of an entire college or university as a physical and intellectual space created to educate women—and women alone—creates a dynamic different from that of a women's center at a coeducational school or a community-based women's center. In either of those cases, the center is a women-only oasis in a larger, mixed-gender world. At a women's college, a women's center (or women's studies department or women's day commemoration) exists within a context that is already dedicated to women's empowerment. It has a concentrating effect. While this effect could be considered redundant or unnecessary, it can also be seen as a distillation and concentration of the most empowering elements of a women's higher education institution.

This question of redundancy raises questions about the necessity of women's colleges and universities in what some people claim is a "postfeminist" world. An argument for their continued need lies in part in each of the four roles I have described so far (access, campus climate, leadership development, gender empowerment). While the trend in most nations in which the majority of students are women is away from single-sex education, in none of these societies is there true gender equity in governance, employment, or family structures. Women's colleges and universities serve as a reminder that gender empowerment is an incomplete agenda, and they provide a number of programs, services, and activities to work toward achieving it.

CHAPTER SEVEN

Women's Colleges and Universities as Symbols, Contradictions, and Paradoxes

----

Hamako, a faculty member in education, showed me into the main building at one of Japan's two national women's universities. "The original campus of [National Women's University] was in a different ward in the city, and after the earthquake and fire we rebuilt the campus here. This was the first building on the new campus." We entered a large, wood-paneled meeting room that, she explained, was once a classroom—outfitted as a dining room—for teaching homemaking and etiquette to students. Etiquette lessons are no longer mandatory, but NWU still supports two student organizations dedicated to learning etiquette and tea ceremony procedures. Students also have the opportunity to participate in dozens of other clubs, including twenty different sports, three of which are martial arts.

Ritual and symbols are important in Japanese culture, Hamako told me, as are hierarchy and order. NWU takes enormous pride in its status as the first higher education institution for Japanese women. It was founded in 1875 as a normal school to educate teachers, survived the 1923 Great Kanto Earthquake, and emerged after World War II as a women's university with faculties in letters, science, and home economics. Hamako offered her interpretation:

NWU is a metaphor of women's strength through the earthquake, fire, and war. No matter the struggles, Japanese women were steady . . . Because we have been through all of that, when they made us a national university it was the right decision.

Being named a national university in 2004 was a substantial landmark in NWU's history and contemporary placement among Japan's leading universities. It also acknowledged, according to Hamako, "The importance of women's education to Japan."

Meeting in her office later in the day, Hamako explained a tension she saw in NWU's priorities:

There is science, we are supposed to emphasize science, and our students and faculty are very good. There is traditional female fields. We have many students in education, home economics. And there is gender studies. We offer a PhD in interdisciplinary gender studies, and the gender studies institute is here . . . Of the three points of the triangle [science, traditional fields, gender studies], it is not clear how they all fit together. They are our past [education / home economics] and today's priority [science], but it is not clear how they make one whole triangle.

I asked if she saw that as a problem, or challenging, for the institution. She said,

It is a tension, keeping ryōsai kenbo *together with science and women's progress. It is nearly impossible to live today if the wife does not also work, so we may need to think differently about "good wife, wise mother." Maybe today to be "good wife" means to have a good job, make a good salary. But she will still have to go home and do the work there.*

Hamako escorted me to my final meeting of the day, a student leadership seminar in which I had been asked to speak about women's leadership in US colleges and universities. The seminar was part of NWU's award-winning multimodal leadership training program that included lectures, seminars, courses, mentoring, and on- and off-campus internship opportunities. After my short presentation, when I opened for discussion, a student spoke of her admiration for then–US Secretary of State Hillary Clinton, saying,

She is a model for me as a woman leader. Her college—the famous Wellesley College—was started the same year as NWU, so I feel there is like a sister college, and when people think of Hillary Clinton and Wellesley College they can think also of NWU, which has its place for women leaders in Japan. When they see us, that can be what they think: women leaders in Japan.

The access, campus climate, leadership, and gender empowerment roles that women's colleges and universities play in the twenty-first century are to varying extents concrete, measurable phenomena. The fifth role that I identified is more abstract but no less real. Women's higher education institutions operate as symbols, enact contradictions, and embody paradoxes. These symbols, contradictions, and paradoxes in turn prompt questions about contemporary women's lives, work, and education. The questions—and their answers—are inherently bound to local contexts, though some have implications across cultural, national, and regional contexts.

Historically, higher education institutions—colleges, universities, institutes, and seminaries—have held symbolic value in their communities. The early history of European universities reveals that the establishment of a university in Cambridge was in part a symbolic move to compete with the city of Oxford; the French recognized the prestige of having a university in Bologna, then established their own university in Paris; and founding "modern" (meaning Western-style) universities in Istanbul, Tokyo, and postindependence Accra, Makarere, Mumbai, and Nairobi symbolically enhanced local honor (see Perkin, 2006). As whites moved west to take up farming across North America, they regarded colleges as symbols of legitimacy for their small towns—never mind that some of these so-called colleges educated fewer than a dozen students, none of whom had completed secondary education (see Thelin, 2011). A sense of pride and boosterism accompanied the opening of these colleges, and sent a signal that their home communities were thriving (even if they were not, or barely so; see Church & Sedlak, 1976).

In addition to acting as symbols of prosperity and pride, colleges and universities are symbols of social change and espoused values. Raj (2012) noted "The mammoth exercise of development of Higher Education in India was taken up shortly after Independence in 1947. The nascent democracy, under the leadership of scholar-Prime Minister, Nehru, believed in idealistic goals of Universities as symbols of progress, humanism and tolerance" (p. 33). In a study of fifteen countries in central and eastern Europe, sub-Saharan Africa, central Asia, and Latin America, Brennan, King, and Lebeau (2004) found that "universities have frequently been regarded as key institutions in processes of social change and development" (p. 7). Furthermore, "especially during periods of more radical change," they play "roles in the building of new institutions of civil society, in encouraging and facilitating new cultural values, and in training and socialising members of new social elites" (p. 7). Within multinational NGOs, higher education is both a development strategy and a symbol of progress; increasing access to tertiary education is a means to an end, and measuring increased access has become a symbol of progress (International Bank for Reconstruction and Development and the World Bank, 2011; UNESCO, n.d.; United Nations Development Programme, 2013).

Specific to women's education, measuring women's participation in higher education is a symbolic marker for progress toward gender equality (see Stromquist, 1990). As I described in chapters 3 and 6, women's access to college is a somewhat recent development in the longer history of higher education and was achieved in the context of fraught public debate about whether women can or should be educated alongside men. Gaining access was at first a largely symbolic victory, as only a relative handful of women were able to matriculate wherever this victory was achieved. But matriculate they did, until the presence of women in higher education became so commonly accepted in most regions as to raise questions about the necessity of having separate colleges and universities for them.

In chapter 6, I described the contributions of women's colleges and universities to gender empowerment through symbols, but here I also ask the following questions: *Have they become symbols of a day gone by? Do they reinforce notions of women as somehow deficient and unable to succeed in a mixed-gender environment?* In their analysis of women's education in Saudi Arabia, for example, Jamjoom and Kelly (2013) argued, "as a cultural symbol, the establishment of an all-women's university further entrenches the notion that women should be cloistered from men" (p. 121). And many scholars and activists believe that higher education as a whole is part of an educational system that perpetuates inequality, regardless of inclusion of historically marginalized groups (for a classic analysis, see Bourdieu & Passeron, 1990). Brennan, King, and Lebeau (2004) summarized this phenomenon in their multinational study: "As far as *social* role is concerned, universities probably contribute quite as much to social reproduction as they do to social transformation" (p. 7). I argue that women's colleges and universities operate as symbols, but they also embody symbolic and actual contradictions and paradoxes while reproducing inequalities of gender, race, social class, caste, and more.

Women's Colleges and Universities as Symbols

That women's colleges and universities exist at all posits them in a symbolic space within society in general and higher education in particular. Their existence takes on meanings beyond what happens on campus. They operate as symbolic reminders that gender equality is not yet achieved and that women's education is a way to move toward it. In chapter 6, I described the ways that institutions contributed to gender empowerment through symbols. But they played additional roles as symbols of educational possibilities, progress, and resistance.

In regions where single-sex education is commonplace or in which many families consider it the only option for their daughters (India, Kenya, Middle

East), the existence of women's colleges and universities signals that girls can and should have high expectations for themselves, that they *can* go on to college and into the workforce. As McDaniel (2010) hypothesized, "Besides the possibility of future opportunities for tertiary enrollment, women's actual opportunities for higher education should positively influence young girls' expectations" (p. 32), a finding she found to be true in many contexts.

When I asked what would happen if there were no women's colleges in the UAE, a student at MEWC said,

> *Girls would not set their goals very high in school. Even if they do not end up coming to college, girls know that MEWC and [a national women's university] are here. They know that some girls do go past high school. So maybe they work harder in school in order to get here.*

A faculty member voiced a similar idea, saying, "Not every girl in the Emirates will go to higher education. But they know we are here. They know that higher education is *possible* for women. We are a symbol of what is possible." Activities like on-campus sports, international tours, preprofessional internships, the student-run campus store, and the annual bazaar were additional symbols of what was possible for women in a rapidly changing society. The rector noted, "Thousands of our alumnae have taken their places in the Emirati workforce. And they are good at what they do. Employers look for our graduates. A degree or diploma from MEWC means something." It means, he explained, that women are capable of higher education and workforce participation, which was not widely believed when the college opened in 1989. "Our alumnae stand for women's potential and for women's accomplishments in the UAE."

In India, the two elite colleges and the comprehensive university I visited operated as symbols in society as a whole and in the higher education ecosystem. Since its founding as a school for widows in a society that shunned them, UCU has been a symbol of women's rights. Its active adult education program and distance education curriculum for students who cannot attend in person signify an ongoing commitment to women learning across the lifespan. A faculty leader noted,

> *Across our [conducted, autonomous, and affiliated] colleges we have the full spectrum from nonformal courses to the PhD. When people see that, I think they may recognize the diversity of women's experiences and educational needs. We have every type of student—highly qualified girls who could go anywhere, working women who are returning for degrees, untrained women who want just a bit more for themselves and their*

families, to PhD students doing advanced research. We are a microcosm of women's
lives in India today. It is important for people to see that diversity.

With its 70,000 students, UCU was a vehicle through which the diversity of Indian women's lives became visible, and its programs and students symbolized women's efforts toward education and self-improvement.

In a different way, the two elite colleges also symbolized women's educational efforts and achievements. These two colleges embodied the ideal that women were fully capable of achieving to the highest academic standards. With nationally ranked academic programs, they demonstrated that women's colleges could compete with men's and coeducational institutions—a sign that their graduates could compete (and win) as well. "No one questions the quality of our degree or our students. It's just assumed that EC girls are the intellectual peer of any man from [elite coeducational college]," said one executive leader. She continued, "I knew that before I came to work here, and now that I know the students and the faculty, I see that it is true." The elite colleges symbolized educational excellence for women.

These institutions also operated symbolically within a network of elite colleges founded under colonial rule, which adds a layer of complexity to understanding their role in women's empowerment. I carefully asked students, faculty, and leaders if they thought there was any tension between being part of this elite network and advocating gender equality. For the most part, they did not see a tension, explaining as one student did, "We must get to [gender] equality in each level of society." Her elite college education would help her "get to equality" within her "level of society," but was not intended (in her mind) to question or alter those levels. To an outsider with an eye for such matters, however, the two elite colleges were symbols of a certain kind of education and social reproduction. A faculty member at UCU—a graduate of an elite women's college I did not visit—noted, "I do see how the [elite] colleges, and even we at UCU, which is more accessible but still not completely open, play a part in the system of haves and have-nots. It is something left from the British system, which we continue." Asked how she felt about the role of elite institutions perpetuating social divides while advocating women's equality, she said,

> But you must also see that in India, there are so many more people—men and women—who want to go to university than there are available places, there is no way to provide any higher education without leaving out hundreds of thousands of the most talented students. Compared to those hundreds of thousands, the thousands who go to

[the elite schools] are a very small part. For what [elite women's colleges] represent in terms of gender equality, it is more important to keep them in a flawed system than to let the system run without them.

According to this line of thinking, closing down elite women's colleges in the name of equity would not quickly resolve the complexity of India's challenges with stratification by class, caste, ethnicity, religion, and gender. They were too important as symbols of gender equality to sacrifice for the purpose of interrupting education's role in social reproduction. Women's colleges and universities around the world operated within complex contexts like this one, and they could be symbols of a number of things—some of them apparently contradictory—at the same time. To insiders, they were symbols of women's talent and potential. But they could also be symbols of old-fashioned gender segregation and regarded as institutions complicit in perpetuating systems of racial, religious, caste, and social class inequality. The extent to which they expressed and dealt with—or even were aware of—these apparently contradictory symbolic roles varied.

Contradictions within Roles and Activities

Because of their particular mission to educate for gender equity and empowerment, women's colleges and universities operate within multiple social and political systems, which results sometimes in what appear to be contradictory roles, activities, and stances. As higher education institutions, they operate within policy frameworks that may require that they act in traditionally masculine ways (e.g., competitive, individualistic). As organizations dedicated to the advancement of women's education, they often at the same time embrace traditionally feminine values (e.g., caring, compassionate, nurturing). While making the case for gender equality, they are components of a larger educational system that perpetuates inequalities. They may espouse culturally located versions of feminism but act in nonfeminist (or anti-feminist) ways. These contradictions occur not only within women's colleges and universities, but also in higher education institutions of different types around the world. But understanding some of the apparent contradictions exhibited among the institutions in this study helps illuminate the contemporary role of women's colleges and institutions.

A purposeful contrariness—perhaps a form of resistance—seems to be behind some apparent contradictions. One example is the alumnae or "old girls'" network at several of the colleges and universities in the study. Students, faculty, and leaders of these institutions have decried the "old boys'" networks of men's institutions that for generations have kept women out of power and influence in society. For example, I learned that the neighboring men's college to the Australian college I visited had produced multiple prime ministers (PMs) and other leaders of society. An institutional leader told me,

> *[Name of men's college] is fiercely closed off to women. And why not? They've got generations of men in power—in government, business, what have you—and they're not about to let that slip . . . We know they [look out for one another], and we work with our girls and alumnae to do the same. Women need to know that it's ok to do that, too. The "old girls" need to stick together.*

Imitating the old boys' network through its alumnae had paid off for AWC in cultivating leaders and helping them achieve success in a number of public arenas. But was there something perhaps contradictory in imitating the very system of exclusion and elitism that AWC was also working against? "Until it's a fair game, we need to do both. We need to copy their strategies *and* fight the good fight against the patriarchy," said the faculty member, "When we've had as many women PMs and [High Court] justices as that college alone, then we might reconsider." In Canada, Italy, Japan, and South Korea, I heard of similar efforts to counter patriarchal structures by cultivating social capital through alumnae networks, though few examples were as explicit. These institutions were appropriating a strategy against which they were also fighting.

Another apparent contradiction that emerged in examining women's colleges and universities was the simultaneous expression of such messages as "we're unique as women's institutions" and "we're just like coeducational institutions." These messages were occasionally delivered at the same time from the same entity, as when I observed a vice president say to Korean Women's University alumnae that KWU "holds a distinctive place in our nation today. We lead the nation in producing women scientists because we know the distinctive needs of women students for the highest quality education and nurturance." In the same speech she said, "There is nothing that sets us apart from the best universities in the world." Most of the time, however, these contradictions emerged from patterns of communication by, to, and among students, faculty, and leaders. A student in China said, for example, "We are no different from the mixed universities. We work just as hard as students at [nearby coeducational universities]." Other students in the focus group nodded their heads in apparent agreement. Yet they also nodded in agreement later, when another student said, "I think if there were boys here we would have to work harder because teachers would expect more from us."

It is possible for both claims to be true: women's colleges and universities are unique *and* they are the same as other postsecondary institutions. What I am calling a contradiction may be a function of strategic messaging or competing beliefs within a community. Women's colleges may simultaneously claim distinctiveness in contexts in which the majority of institutions are coeducational, and they may assert that they are like coeducational peer institutions in many of their structures and functions.

The women's colleges and universities played out apparent contradictions in other symbolic forms, too. Below I describe their paradoxical stance as agents of gender empowerment and maintainers of the status quo. In terms of simple contradictions, however, I offer the examples of campus life policies and of the curriculum. In chapter 4, I described the elite Catholic college in India, which women fully occupied with noise and bright colors. This apparent freedom contrasted with a strict 8:00 p.m. curfew in the on-campus hostel. On campus, women could express themselves more freely, vocally, and visibly than outside the college gates, but larger social concerns about safety and values related to reputation (the students' and the college's) resulted in the contradictory message that women were unsafe and not to be trusted to themselves in the evening. One student offered, "They treat us like young girls in the hostel but want us to be these women leaders. How does that make sense?" MEWC students could exercise their freedom to drive to the campus, but they could not leave during the day without permission from their parents (or husbands). Japanese institutions sponsored gender research centers but also emphasized the role of women in traditional roles (as wives, homemakers, early childhood educators), including at one an elective course in traditional Japanese etiquette.

Another interpretation of these apparent contradictions is not through an either/or binary but through a both/and construction. It is possible both to be feminist (or feminine) *and* to operate within masculinist structures of public policy and higher education systems. The principal of the Canadian women's college described how she incorporated the feminist decision-making style she inherited from the Ursuline tradition of the college into a distinctly hierarchical structure of the secular, public university in which the college was located:

> We operate on a consensus model up to the Council [of Trustees] level. When meeting
> to make important decisions, we will discuss at the first meeting and come to a sense
> of our decision. But we don't make the decision then. We wait for the next meeting,
> so that there is time for different ideas to percolate, for someone to have and voice second
> thoughts, for thoughtful discernment before finalizing an important decision . . .

It takes a bit longer than just taking a vote in the first place. But I think we make bet-ter decisions this way.

Asked how the consensus model of the women's college worked within the hierarchical context of the university as a whole, the principal laughed and said, "Well, a lot of it comes down to me in between the two ways of working. I feel comfortable in both, though it can be hard to explain the one to the other some-times." She embraced her role in the "both/and" to operate within competing, if not contradictory, modes of institutional leadership. This experience reflected Stromquist's (2001a) summary of the situation of women's studies programs in patriarchal universities: "Through women's and gender studies, women have gained new and relatively autonomous spaces within the university. Ironically, these programs operate under the same patriarchal dependent conditions affect-ing women in the rest of society" (p. 382). The Canadian residential college thus operated with some autonomy and feminist principles within the context of the university as a whole.

Another apparent contradiction emerged in the ways that women's colleges and universities promoted gender equality yet were implicated in the reproduc-tion of unequal power structures in society. The highly selective colleges and universities I studied in Australia, China, India, Japan, South Korea, and the United Kingdom certainly played a role in perpetuating the role of elites in those societies. By activating their old girls' networks, they created a class of educated women who were prepared to enter positions of power, even if they still faced sexism and other barriers on their way and once there.

A few of the institutions I studied engaged in employment practices that took advantage of the local labor market in ways that could seem less than equita-ble. For example, they treated (and paid) adjunct instructors poorly because, as a (male) adjunct instructor in Kenya told me, "They know we cannot get a per-manent teaching job elsewhere, so they can pay us very little. But what can we do?" In India, Kenya, and the UAE, members of locally marginalized groups or immigrants performed custodial, cooking, and serving tasks. A faculty member in India told me that although these staff were treated "better than they would be off campus" serving in similar roles, many students and faculty from higher castes ignored them or treated them as servants.

No, the daughters of the drivers and canteen workers are not likely to come to our col-lege as students. They would be very welcome once they proved themselves on the en-trance exam, but it is very unlikely that their parents can yet afford the schools neces-

sary to get them to our level. But they might go to other good colleges, and maybe their
children would have the chance.

Attitudes about affirmative action (also called "reservation") for members
of underrepresented groups in higher education likewise reflected contradictions related to fighting for gender equality while perpetuating other forms of
inequalities. Majority students in Australia, India, and the United Kingdom
expressed both sympathy for the idea of diversifying the student population and
concerns about the "fairness" of a reservation system that could, as one student
put it, "admit someone less qualified over someone more qualified, just because
she is a minority." I pointed out that in the case of highly selective admissions
processes, such as at these institutions, there must inevitably be a greater number of "qualified" students than there are spaces at the institution, but the student insisted that "some girls admitted under quota really ought not have made
it in." I did not point out that these same arguments were often made about
admitting women to coeducational institutions.

In an international analysis of the incorporation of women into higher education (regardless of the gender composition of their institutions), Bradley (2000)
concluded that higher education exists "at the nexus of status-competition and
status-equality efforts, provid[ing] a lens for examining attempts to transform
gender relations in society" (p. 10). This claim partially explains some of what
I observed on campuses. A college degree is valuable and brings status in professional, family, and personal life (see McMahon, 2009, for an international
analysis). The more prestigious the degree-granting institution, the more potential social capital the student accrues. But even less prestigious institutions con-
fer status on the graduate, particularly in contexts in which access to higher education remains elusive for large numbers of individuals who cannot find seats in
their home country or afford to go abroad. Institutions maintain their prestige
in part by participating in a system that relies on scarcity and competition—
the scarcity of seats in the entering class and consequent competition for those
seats. In this context, working toward equality across multiple categories (e.g.,
race, ethnicity, class, caste) is difficult.

The women's colleges and universities in this study were, for the most part,
focused on the goal of increasing women's progress in educational status and
women's equality, sometimes at the expense of broader equality agendas. Two
exceptions were MEWC and UCU, which invested in activities such as adult
education and workforce training, broadening access to women from diverse
life circumstances. They had not fully resolved contradictions related to the pur-

suit of equality, but they were a bit closer than most of the other institutions in the study.

Yuval-Davis (2011) takes a global perspective on the question of intersectionalities of gender, social class, race/ethnicity, religion, nationality, and so forth. In the United States, intersectionality emerged from the work of women of color scholar-activists, and Crenshaw (1991) laid a foundation for it in critical legal studies. Among others, Collins (2000) and Dill and Zambrana (2009) have extended the concept. An underlying principle of all of this writing is that it is unwise—indeed impossible—to disentangle racialized, gendered, and classed experiences because they are mutually constituting. At the women's colleges and universities I studied, awareness of gender was high, but awareness of intersectional lives and experiences was lower, in some cases almost nonexistent. Faculty seemed more aware than students, and gender studies scholars the most aware of all. Future studies could explore this topic more fully to understand complexities within institutions and national systems of higher education.

The Paradox of Symbolizing Gender Equity and Status Quo

Just as they exhibit a number of apparently contradictory stances, as a group and individually, women's institutions operate paradoxically as symbols of gender equity and symbols of traditional gender norms. As I noted in chapter 3, they celebrated pioneering women and provided leadership training to students whom they expected to "be the best" and "change the world." They also perpetuated stereotypes of women as needing protection, preparing to be "good wives and wise mothers," and learning to be assertive but not too much. Two strong themes from the study combine to support my claim about the paradoxical symbolic role of women's institutions: women's institutions as progressive organizations and women's institutions as perpetuators of gender stereotypes. In all the national contexts I examined, women's institutions existed in a paradoxical symbolic space where they operate simultaneously as progressive and conservative organizations.

Women's Institutions as Progressive Organizations

As described in chapter 6, women's college and universities act as progressive organizations that promote gender equality in their local context. In some cases (noted in chap. 3), they provided higher education access to women who, by policy (as in the UAE) or in cultural and family practice (as in parts of India and Kenya), cannot attend higher education in mixed-gender settings. A faculty leader in the UAE said, "I'm so proud of what we've done in creating a place that produces female college graduates who go on to public roles in a society that by and large keeps women out of sight." Well-publicized visits from high-ranking public officials and visiting dignitaries also emphasized the symbolic role of these institutions in societies that have a long way to go in moving toward gender equality.

Even where women outnumber men in undergraduate enrollments and enjoy full access to higher education, women's institutions act symbolically to remind society that in many other domains of public and private life, gender equality remains elusive. As described in chapter 6, women's studies programs and gender studies research centers were common features of the women's institutions I studied. A faculty researcher at one of these centers in Japan noted that people often ask her why a women's university needs a women's research institute, explaining, "But no one at the mixed [gender] universities will do the work that needs to be done!" Indeed, the *only* women's studies undergraduate major in China is at one of the country's three women's institutions. The very fact that women's institutions exist at all in highly developed educational systems raises questions—such as *Why would you want to work/go* there?—that faculty and students said gave them opportunities to discuss gender inequality in society. A Canadian student who described herself as a feminist said, "Every time one of my cousins or their friends asks me why I chose a women's college, my sister rolls her eyes, because she knows what I'll say next about gender inequality and women's place in society." Standing as symbols against gender inequality, women's institutions act progressively as reminders that all is not yet resolved when it comes to gender in society.

A third way that these institutions acted progressively for gender equity was in providing explicit training for students as future women leaders (chap. 4). Through institutional slogans and branding (an international phenomenon in countries where competition for students is strong), students learned that they were expected to "make a difference," "go where others will not go," be "women for the world," and "learn, serve, lead." Whether out of genuine concern for student development (I met with many institutional leaders, faculty, and staff who seemed sincere in these efforts) or a need to position a single-sex institution in a challenging student recruiting environment, leadership education was a staple in these women's institutions. Students pointed out the ways that they were able to—indeed had to—take up all leadership roles on campus, which they believed prepared them for taking up leadership roles in society. Institutions touted alumnae who have become leaders in government, industry, and civic life. A persistent message across countries was that women's institutions are not simply training women to lead in college, they are preparing women to lead in society—a progressive stance in every country in the study. Symbolically, women's institutions operated as incubators of and launching grounds for female leadership and gender equality.

Women's Institutions Perpetuate Gender Stereotypes

At the same time that they promoted gender equity, women's institutions perpetuated gender stereotypes and separate spheres. Women's institutions acted in ways that symbolically reinforced gender stereotypes. The theme of protecting women (often called "girls") came up at several institutions, for example. Protection sometimes took the form of physical isolation and restricting access (e.g., locating campuses remotely, fencing or gating them even when nearby coeducational campuses had open access). Hostels (residence halls) had parietal rules with curfews and strict "lights out" times. Faculty at one campus talked about not overstressing "our girls" with too much homework, and at the Kenyan campus one (male) professor noted that he sends "the girls away [from the math major] if they struggle too much" because he does not want them to be "heartbroken from learning." Echoing the debates about women's higher education from generations past, these students needed protection because they were weak or at risk.

The notion of "Republican motherhood" (Palmieri, 1987) or "good wife, wise mother" (known as *ryōsai kenbo* in Japan; see McVeigh, 1997; Shizuko, 2012) persists in women's higher education institutions. That is, the reason that women should be educated is to enhance their ability to be a good wife, homemaker, and mother. Rooted in the nineteenth and early twentieth centuries in Western societies and exported to Asia and elsewhere, this idea holds that a woman's role exists largely in the private sphere of home and community life, not in the workforce. Higher education should therefore prepare her for a life of service to husband, family, and community. Several faculty in Japan and Korea, in particular, noted the economic reality that most female university graduates would need to be part of the workforce until retirement age, even while they were expected to bear the large majority of home and family responsibilities. Vestiges of the "good wife, wise mother" philosophy, on which several Asian women's institutions were founded, remain in the curriculum. Although they emphasized their contributions in STEM fields, for example, the Japanese national university enrolled a preponderance of its students in fields traditionally studied by women, such as education and home economics, and students organized two clubs that offered lessons in traditional and highly gendered etiquette. Campus life was also heavily focused on activities that were consistent with *ryōsai kenbo*. Students described a number of extracurricular activities that promoted hetero-sexual dating with a view toward marriage, as well as lessons in manners and hospitality. One said,

> It is well known that graduates of our college make good wives for businessmen. It is
> an advantage for a man to marry one of us if he wants to succeed. And of course if he
> succeeds, we are happy!

Students at elite and nonelite institutions in India spoke openly about the ways that a university education enhanced their value on the marriage market, even though most of them believed that their own marriage would be based on other factors. Women's institutions in India and elsewhere were seen as places that ensured the virtue of female students by both protecting them from unwanted sexual attention or assault and preventing them from choosing romantic alli-ances with men their families would deem inappropriate. "My parents will let me make a love match, but it must be with a boy from the right family, with a good education, or else my mother will make an arrangement," said a student at one of the elite colleges. "My CCM education will be an advantage, because his fam-ily will know that I am hardworking and have not been around boys very much."

With few exceptions, these institutions opened their campuses to outsiders and in every case employed men as faculty and staff. Even at the Canadian wom-en's college—which once contained a convent for the order of founding Catholic sisters—the idea of a convent-like enclosure keeping (presumably) dangerous men out of women's colleges was a myth. But this myth did create the opportu-nity for women from some conservative families to attend college. As noted in chapter 3, in India, Kenya, and the UAE, many students reported that their fami-lies would not have allowed them to leave home to attend a coeducational college. With their virtue—and thus bridal value—assured, they were permitted to pur-sue higher education under the condition that it occurred in an institution that promised safety for women's bodies, minds, souls, and reputations.

Women's institutions remained locations for the promotion of traditional values and gender roles. A faculty member in gender studies at Japan's NWU pointed out the ways that the university had always been an officially sanctioned mediator of women's roles. Teaching or homemaking were acceptable vocations; scientific research, law, or medicine were not. "And still, we have tension—like a three-way pull—between STEM, gender studies, and traditional female fields. We *say* we are about STEM and maybe gender studies, but underneath is a strong current of traditional fields," she said. Her students proudly pointed out that the university had historical ties to the empress, including at the time of my visit a role for the university's kindergarten in educating a member of the royal family. Students seemed unconcerned that their university was more popularly known for its kindergarten than its undergraduate science programs. A strong undercurrent of *ryōsai kenbo* was alive and well in this twenty-first-century women's university in Japan.

Women's institutions thus sustained a paradoxical culture of both empowering women and protecting them from outside forces. Faculty spoke of protecting "the girls" while teaching them skills and knowledge to engage in professions previously closed to women. A student services staff person in China taught women how to be assertive leaders yet not lose their femininity and appeal to potential mates. Italian students followed the example of their stylish rector to develop intellectual sharpness, leadership, and entrepreneurialism while maintaining acceptable feminine grace. Some campuses (e.g., in the UAE) were tightly secured against outsiders yet promoted the value of engaging in community service and workplace internships as a means of professional and personal development. In Kenya, KIST faculty protected "our girls" from too much stress while preparing them to be pioneers in STEM fields.

The paradox extended to preserving traditional values while promoting social change and gender equity. *Because* of this paradox, Muslim students at CCM could enter their gated campus, hang up their burqas, take up space with sound and color and movement, read texts both traditional and radical, and then return home to their communities, where they lived mainly out of sight of the fathers, uncles, and husbands who would make decisions about their lives. As the rector of MEWC said,

> We create a space where women can come and learn. We can't control what they do with what they learn once they leave at the end of the day or the end of their program. But we can hope. We can hope.

Hope for what? "Hope that by working within the culture as it is today we can create more options for women and girls tomorrow." What appeared to be a paradox from one perspective could be seen from another as a strategy for gradual social change.

Summary

Adding to the more observable roles of access, campus climate, leadership development, and gender empowerment, women's colleges and universities in the twenty-first century acted as symbols in society generally and in the educational system in particular. They also embodied contradictions and paradox. This symbolic, contradictory, and paradoxical state seemed to bring about an awareness in some students, faculty, and leaders that these institutions had a meaning in their local contexts that went beyond simply being one more college or university in the system. Even accounting for the likelihood that familiarity, affection, and loyalty played a part in how the people I met felt and thought about their institutions, there was a sense of exceptionalism about the role that women's colleges and universities played.

The institutions in this study act as symbols of what is possible for girls and women. Even in Kenya, with its one relatively new and very small private women's university, the presence of "a college of one's own" (Hasan, 2008) drew attention to the potential—perhaps even the expectation—that girls will continue through secondary school into college. A college of one's own also symbolizes the expectation that women will do something with the education they receive. Why would a woman study chemistry or engineering or computer science if she were not going to be a chemist, an engineer, or a computer scientist? Within the symbolic space of higher education, women's institutions occupy a niche that sends messages to girls, women, and society.

Women's institutions also embodied contradictions. They were, to some people, fundamentally about creating gender equality, yet they operated within systems of education that perpetuated other inequalities. Elite institutions particularly illustrated this phenomenon, but no colleges or universities that I studied were immune to it. Women's colleges and universities claimed uniqueness yet also claimed to be "just like" their coeducational peers. Some espoused feminist values while organizing and operating in masculinist ways. To be clear, I do not view contradictions as a sign of weakness, disarray, or confused messaging. They are rather signs that women's colleges and universities in the twenty-first century are—like coeducational institutions—complex organizations with competing and contradictory internal cultures and external portrayals. They are "both/and" organizations rather than "either/or" ones.

They also entailed paradox. At the center of their paradoxical roles of progressivism and conservatism lies the reality that in every case, women's colleges and universities are in some way countercultural. In national contexts where coeducation is the overwhelming norm (e.g., Australia, Canada, China, Japan, Kenya, South Korea), it is countercultural to maintain set-aside space for women's education. Where single-sex education is normative if not universal (e.g., India, UAE), it is also countercultural—to at least some substantial part of the population—to provide any formal higher education to women.

Women's colleges and universities, in this paradoxical state, highlight their historic and contemporary roles as countercultural institutions. No longer only about access (in most places), they remain essential for access for *some* women. Pressing a progressive agenda for gender equity, they operate (in some places) in the interstitial spaces of society where women are allowed to learn and to know, but not in public, which is men's space (see Phadke, Khan, & Ranade, 2011, for an analysis of gender and public space). Where any higher education for women is countercultural, the private spaces of women's colleges and universities are simultaneously liberatory and protective. Yet also, where separate higher education for women is countercultural, the private spaces of women's institutions raise questions about gender equity and the proper role of women in society. The paradox—the countercultural existence—of women's colleges and universities plays a symbolic role in national systems of education and higher education. It draws attention to what has been, what is, and what might be.

CHAPTER EIGHT

Raising Questions in the Present and about the Future

The women's colleges and universities featured in this study were neither finishing schools nor cloistered convents, and they all clearly played roles in contemporary society and in higher education systems. Still, the existence of women's colleges and universities in a world that, in the vast majority of contexts, legally permits women to attend mixed-gender institutions, which in turn educate the vast majority of female college students, raises a question. *Do we really still have women's colleges?* Yes, we do, especially when looking outside the United States, but that answer raises two more questions. *Why? What are they for?*

I concluded on the basis of what I learned that women's institutions play the five roles discussed in previous chapters. They provide access, particularly for women who face ongoing cultural barriers to attending higher education in mixed-gender environments. They create a campus climate that is particularly friendly to women, one that lacks the overt sexual harassment and discrimination at coeducational institutions. They cultivate women as leaders. They promote a culture of gender empowerment. And they act as symbols of women's potential and achievements, while also displaying contradictions and paradoxes that persist in societies in which gender equality is not yet achieved.

Questions about Education and Society

Overlying all of these roles, the countercultural presence of women-only institutions raises the question of why they exist. In regions where women predominate at coeducational institutions, why does anyone need women's colleges? In regions where women are not allowed to attend coeducational institutions or to take up a career after college, what is the point in educating women at all? As examined in chapter 7, women's institutions operate symbolically to raise these questions. The answers varied across regions, but in every case, women's colleges and universities prompted similar questions.

Why would a woman choose a woman-only institution?

As in the United States, women's institutions in Australia, Canada, China, Italy, Japan, Kenya, South Korea, and the United Kingdom are not typical choices for female students. As such, they cause outsiders—and sometimes their own students and faculty—to question their existence. The answers come in formal communications (e.g., promotional materials, alumnae communiqués, websites, DVDs, admissions publications) and informal formats (e.g., social networking sites, unofficial blogs, student newspapers). Existing literature presented throughout this book points to the ways that women's colleges and universities outperform coeducational institutions in providing access to positive academic and extracurricular environments for female students. A particular emphasis on STEM and other subjects (law, business, medicine) not traditionally studied by women is a hallmark of many women's colleges and universities. Additional reasons women chose single-sex higher education relate to finances (some women's institutions are more affordable than coeducational options), admissions criteria (most of the institutions I studied have slightly to somewhat less rigorous standards for admission than their coeducational peers), specialized curriculum (women's studies, STEM, health professions), and a desire to develop leadership skills. Finally, culture and family constrained some students' choices, most notably in the UAE and India.

What is happening at coeducational schools that makes women's institutions preferred choices for some students?

It seemed from my interviews and focus groups with students, faculty, and institutional leaders that the decision to attend a women's college or university is for many students a decision *not* to attend a coeducational one. My study did not directly compare women's institutions to mixed-gender or men's schools, but there are a number of existing studies that document and analyze women's experiences at coeducational universities. I also learned a lot from faculty who had experience at coeducational universities and about students' perceptions—gained through traditional and social media or from peer networks—of the climate for women and experiences of female students in formerly men's colleges and historically coeducational institutions.

A "chilly climate" for women in the classroom and on the rest of campus (Hall & Sandler, 1982, 1984) persists to varying degrees around the world (Gunawardena, Rasanayagam, Leitan, Bulumulle, & Abeyasekera-Van Dort, 2006; Kwesiga & Ssendiwala, 2006; Morley, 2006a, 2011; Morrison, Bourke, & Kelley, 2005; Mukhopadhyay, 2004; Najar, 2013; Odejide, Akanji, & Odekunle, 2006; Wall, 2008). The behaviors reported range from "just" being ignored or passed over in favor of men to blatant discrimination, harassment, sexual assault, and other violence. The underrepresentation of women in STEM fields, and the nature of some STEM learning environments (e.g., laboratories), may exacerbate the negative climate for women. Female students and faculty may not only lack role models in these fields, but also they may lack a critical mass of peers with whom they can collaborate, study, socialize, and (if necessary) consult about discriminatory incidents or harassment (Burke & Mattis, 2007; Carrigan, Quinn, & Riskin, 2011; Kim & Sax, 2009; Kodate, Kodate, & Kodate, 2010; National Academies, 2008).

Students and faculty spoke to me of harassment and discrimination that they or their female friends experienced in coeducational undergraduate and graduate STEM classrooms and laboratories. In Japan and Korea, women's college faculty were particularly adamant about the ways that their institutions provided access to high-quality STEM education, free from harassment. The curriculum at the Kenyan institution focused on science and technology because women were treated poorly at the coeducational public universities. Some students in India selected the women's comprehensive university over better-ranked coeducational institutions because they heard from their sisters and friends about harassment (and worse) in coeducational STEM majors.

There are a number of explanations forwarded for why the climate for women at coeducational institutions is not better. It is beyond the scope of this book to describe them in depth, but at the core is the reality that, at this time in history, coeducational institutions fail to provide equitable access to curricular and extracurricular learning opportunities for women. Access to higher education does not mean equity. Admitting women to a formerly men's college or university does not mean that they will be treated fairly, humanely, or well. Would the question about gender climate at coeducational institutions arise without the presence of a single-sex alternative? Very likely—and I certainly hope—it would. Until the campus climate equally favors women and men, however, women's colleges and universities stand as a reminder that there is work yet to be done in coeducational environments.

What is happening at women's colleges and universities that is particularly good?

Women's institutions serve important roles in their local, national, and regional contexts, and they performed several of them particularly well. As well as providing hospitable learning climates, they provide out-of-class opportunities for leadership development and opportunities to which women believe they would not have equal access at coeducational institutions. This belief is widespread among students (see Renn & Lytle, 2010), including those at every institution in this study. There is no empirical evidence that these same women would *not* take up leadership activities at coeducational institutions, but students in every region and institutional type spoke about the ways that they had access to the highest levels of student leadership (e.g., student government, honor councils, student organizations, campus publications, academic societies). They also spoke about realizing that they would not have taken up certain activities—anything from sports to managing student government finances to hauling heavy pieces of equipment for a theatrical production—had men been present.

Faculty and administrators shared this belief in the advantages of single-sex over coeducational settings for the development of women's leadership. In regions where prospective students much less prefer single-sex higher education and women's colleges compete with coeducational schools for talented students (e.g., Australia, Canada, Japan, South Korea, the United Kingdom, the United States), institutional communication, marketing, and branding are particularly forthcoming on this point. In the UAE, where the government-sponsored women's college I visited offered tuition-free education in the much preferred single-sex format, there was less need for branding and marketing, yet the institutional focus on developing students for leadership in all sectors of society was clear and apparently effective.

In addition to academic climate and leadership development, women's colleges and universities provided access to higher education for women who for a number of reasons (policy, finances, academic preparation) would not have been able to attend university, or to attend an institution with a reputation comparable to the single-sex one that became their alma mater. Providing access has always been a key role of women's colleges and universities, but uncovering the ways that gender intersected with culture, social class, and academic preparation showed particularly positive contributions of these institutions. Through financial packages for women from poor families and underrepresented minority students, they also demonstrated a commitment to educating diverse women, which students reported they did not see as a priority at coeducational institutions. To be sure, there is progress yet to be made in diversity at women's colleges and universities, as in coeducational higher education.

Inasmuch as one considers gender empowerment to be of value, there is evidence in this study that women's colleges and universities are effective cultivators of it. Student and alumnae outcomes seem to clearly support this claim. Reports of engagement with local communities of advocates for women and for gender empowerment also indicate that women's colleges and universities perform this role well. Women's studies departments and centers at coeducational institutions may also do well in this area, and the debate is open about whether separate or mixed-gender organizations are most effective in facilitating gender empowerment (Daly, 2005; Unterhalter, 2005; Walby, 2005). That debate is unlikely to be settled any time soon. In the early twenty-first century, gender segregation and gender mainstreaming are in any case happening concurrently among higher education institutions in the countries I visited, and women's colleges seem to be doing a good job promoting gender empowerment.

Can coeducational institutions replicate these supportive conditions and results for women?

Whether one believes that all higher education institutions at some point in the future should be coeducational or that there will always be a role for women's colleges and universities, it is interesting to consider whether and how coeducational institutions could be more hospitable to women. After all, the large majority of female students worldwide attend mixed-gender higher education institutions, and every indication is that this situation will not change; indeed, that majority is likely to increase. As Tidball et al. (1999) asked regarding women's colleges in the United States, I ask whether the lessons of women's colleges and universities can be translated into effective strategies for educating women in coeducational contexts in other nations. I propose that some can but some cannot.

Coeducational institutions in some regions could do more to promote access for female students. Even where truly mixed-gender education is prohibited (e.g., Saudi Arabia), there are recent inroads into allowing women to study in facilities of equal caliber to those available to men, and with the same faculty (Jamjoom & Kelly, 2013; Naidoo & Moussly, 2009). By being creative with organizing curriculum, facilities, and extracurricular offerings (see Lipka, 2012), institutions can maintain culturally appropriate gender segregation while offering women greater access to opportunities than has previously been available.

In regions where educating men and women together is not a barrier to access, coeducational institutions could do more to promote women's access through gender-based affirmative action in admissions and targeted financial awards (e.g., grants, scholarships, fellowships). These measures could counter local effects of unequal precollege preparation for girls and cultural values that prompt some families to favor sons over daughters in education. Outreach through mentoring and tutoring programs that focus on girls—particularly poor girls from minority communities—could be another way that coeducational institutions could increase overall participation of women in higher education, just as the Australian Women's College worked with Aboriginal girls to prepare them for college applications.

Access is important, but improving campus climate is equally so. Women need access not only to higher education, but also to environments that support their learning and development. The literature on improving the gender climate on campus points to several strategies (e.g., having gender-inclusive policies in place and educating staff, faculty, and students about sexual harassment and discrimination), but each of these strategies must also be undertaken in a culturally appropriate way. What works in the UAE may not be appropriate in Canada; what is effective and culturally sound in India may not be in Italy or the United Kingdom.

Looking instead to what the women's colleges and universities do well within their national and cultural contexts could provide some ideas. It is not possible (or even a good idea) for a coeducational institution to eject men and become completely single sex, but creating spaces within the campus for women-only activities might replicate some of the freedom students experienced at women's colleges. For example, it seems possible to create voluntarily gender-segregated physical, intellectual, and social spaces, whether in person or online, in which women could opt to participate. Having a space away from the feeling of constant—and constantly gendered—surveillance could create pockets of the freedom that Jill Ker Conway (2001) observed at Smith College and that I saw in the noisy, colorful, expression of ownership students displayed on the campuses I visited. The programs, services, and facilities of the residential women's colleges within coeducational universities in Australia, Canada, Italy, and the United Kingdom are good examples of this possibility, and may be something for other coeducational universities to consider in some form, whether residential or otherwise.

Positive climates for women extended beyond classrooms and campus space into opportunities for leadership development. Because one feature of the women's college environment that promoted leadership development was the simple fact of having opportunities available, strategies for coeducational institutions could include (in ways appropriate to the local context) reserving spaces for women in leadership, creating leadership development programs aimed at women, and actively encouraging women to become leaders. Role models and mentors were important to the students I encountered during this study and during my previous study of leaders at women's colleges (Renn & Lytle, 2010). An extensive international literature on mentoring points out that men can be effective mentors to women. The responsibility for mentoring need not fall only on female faculty and staff at coeducational institutions. Highlighting the achievements of diverse women leaders in all sectors of society would be another strategy for coeducational institutions to consider.

It is unclear what role coeducational institutions could or might play in gender empowerment generally, though there is no reason to think that their women's studies programs and university women's centers do not make similar contributions to those at women's colleges and universities. There is also no reason that coeducational institutions, particularly those in regions where the minority of college students are female, could not act as symbols for women's educational and career potential by highlighting alumnae and students, hiring more female faculty, and ensuring that institutional leadership includes women who are visible to the public. Coeducational institutions could also support the role of women's colleges in gender empowerment by partnering with them on educational and extracurricular programming that promotes gender equity.

Looking for Clues to the Future in the Present

Along with raising questions about what women's colleges and universities do and how their successes might be replicated at coeducational institutions, my study raises an inevitable question. *What is the future of single-sex postsecondary education worldwide?* The answer depends on understanding an analysis of women's colleges and universities as organizations embedded in global, national, and local policy contexts, as well as being at the intersection of gender, social class, and cultural forces. Coeducational institutions are also embedded in these contexts, but they are less centrally interested in and dependent on gender (and women specifically) in their mission and contributions to society.

Global, National, and Local Influences on Education

I began this project with a question about what roles women's colleges and universities play in the twenty-first century. This book describes and analyzes their roles largely in local and national contexts because, for the individual institutions examined here, they are the most immediate, proximal contexts in the awareness of students, faculty, and most administrators. Yet globalization and multinational NGOs influence the macrocontext of women's colleges and universities. To account for *global*, *national*, and *local* agencies (e.g., NGOs, as well as higher education institutions) and their agency (ability to act), Marginson and Rhoades (2002) proposed a "glonacal agency heuristic." In the glonacal agency heuristic, Marginson and Rhoades "emphasize the interactions, interaction, mutual determinations of these levels (global, national, and local) and domains (organizational agencies and the agency of collectivities)" (p. 289). It is useful to consider women's colleges and universities individually and as a group through this heuristic.

As noted in chapters 1 and 3, a number of global NGOs advocate for women's education as a solution to a host of persistent economic, social, and human rights problems. The United Nations works toward gender equality through education in the UN Development Programme, UNESCO, UN Women, UN Girls' Education Initiative, and Millennium Development Goals, among other initiatives. The World Bank promotes gender equality in development as a key strategy in ending poverty. The OECD Gender Initiative (within the Families and Children section of the Directorate for Employment, Labour, and Social Affairs) includes women's education as both a strategy toward and a measure of women's equality. None of these agencies has, to my knowledge, ever mandated the foundation or continuation of women's colleges and universities. But they influence, particularly in developing regions, national policies and priorities related to girls' and women's education (see Metcalfe, 2011), and that influence translates in some cultural contexts into the promotion of single-sex schools as a means to increase female participation from elementary through postsecondary levels. Inasmuch as progress toward global NGOs' goals for gender equality rests on their work, women's colleges and universities would seem to remain vital organizations for the foreseeable future.

Women's colleges and universities also play a part in global mobility of students, though this effect was not particularly evident on the campuses I visited, which drew nearly all of their students from their home nation. It is more clear in observing enrollment and employment patterns of women's colleges in the United States, which have in the face of declining applications from domestic female students turned to recruiting international students whose families would not consider sending their daughters out of country to coeducational institutions (see Lewin, 2008). International students now constitute one-quarter of

Mount Holyoke College's matriculants, for example, and the admissions office provides information in Arabic, Bengali, Bulgarian, Georgian, Hindi, Japanese, Korean, Mandarin, Nepalese, Portuguese, Spanish, Twi, Urdu, and Vietnamese (Mount Holyoke College Office of Admissions, 2013).

The global mobility of faculty and leaders was more evident at the institutions in my study. In part because I relied in six cases on contacts through the international organization Women's Education Worldwide to enlist participating institutions, I interviewed a number of leaders (rectors, vice chancellors, presidents, principals) who had connections to leaders of women's colleges and universities in other countries. Many of them had earned their doctorates outside the country in which they were now working, as had a number of faculty members; I also met a number of expatriate faculty during my visits. To varying degrees, these educators saw themselves, their institutions, and women's education in global perspective—whether focused on preparing students to deal with international business colleagues, to teach in bilingual refugee-serving elementary schools, or to use gender theory to analyze World Court decisions. These women's colleges and universities were influenced to varying extents both by global agencies and actors within the globalized network of higher education.

Keeping in mind Shahjahan and Kezar's (2013) caution against what they called methodological nationalism, there is still no escaping the fact that higher education institutions operate within national systems of policy, practice, and governance—a fact that is accounted for within the Marginson and Rhoades (2002) glonacal approach. Within their national contexts, the institutions in this study fell into four types: (1) completely private, not directly government funded (Kenya, South Korea, and Suburban College in Japan); (2) completely public, directly government funded or subsidized (China, India's Urban Comprehensive University, Japan's National Women's University, and the UAE); (3) independent constituent or affiliated college of a public university, government funded for student tuition and academic programs (the two elite Indian colleges); and (4) residential college within a public university, government subsidy for student tuition but not college programs (e.g., housing, counseling, tutoring; Australia, Canada, Italy, the United Kingdom). To some extent, these four different types of relationships to and financial dependence on (or independence from) ministries of education influenced the national context for women's colleges and universities and their prospects for the future. In one example, changes in tuition schemes for students at public universities in the United Kingdom were underway when I conducted my study. Increased tuition charges levied by the university would drastically affect the ability of the residential college to attract students from lower-income groups. The national-level effects of the global economic crisis that began in 2009 (just as I was beginning data collection) manifested across institutions in concerns voiced by students and institutional leaders about support for student costs and uncertain labor markets for graduates.

As noted throughout this book, in some contexts women's colleges and universities played a specific, strategic part in national education, economic, and development policies. Increasing girls' and women's education levels has been a recent priority in the Middle East, with such success that women today represent the majority of students in higher education in some countries. Attention is now turning from improving access to supporting other areas of gender empowerment.

> The government of Saudi Arabia has adopted a clear vision for the empowerment of women as reflected in recent development plans that show a clear shift in the orientation of planning efforts towards the development of women's roles instead of focusing on women's right to education and employment . . . The recommendations called for the expansion of women's role, their participation in public endeavours and expression of opinions, an examination of the legal system and its role in empowering women, the separation of traditions and customs from law and religion and the creation of new educational endeavours, both academic and vocational and new work opportunities for women. (Al-Ahmadi, 2011, pp. 149–50)

Although the Kenyan Institute of Science and Technology was new, private, and for profit, Kenya's minister for higher education was exploring the possibility of creating single-sex public higher education options for women in STEM fields. In 2012, the University Grants Commission, which oversees Indian higher education, was promoting the establishment of an additional twenty women's universities and eight hundred women's colleges to address the need for accessible higher education options for women (*Times of India*, 2012). At the national level, policymakers may view women's colleges and universities as strategic agencies in enacting development, economic, educational, and gender empowerment agendas.

Just as important is considering the national context for higher education as a whole and the role of women's colleges within the higher education system. As I have noted in earlier chapters, the relative availability of affordable, academically accessible higher education is a key factor in understanding the role of women's institutions. Where competition for seats in higher education is stiff (e.g., India, China) and women's colleges and universities receive government funding, they add to the available options of affordable education for women. There seems little chance of them failing to fill their entering classes; for example, with an admission rate below 1%, the elite (and government-subsidized) colleges in India are not at risk of closure. But in Kenya, where competition for admission is also fierce, a private university for women with tuition costs much higher than a rural family's annual income does not fare as well in recruiting students who can pay to attend. Certainly many women from these countries, like the international students at Mount Holyoke, pursue an education away from home, but for those families who would not send a daughter abroad to a coeducational institution, single-sex options in Australia, Europe, and North America are rather limited (e.g., the one-quarter of Mount Holyoke students who are international amounts to only about 525 women at a time, spread across four academic class years). Furthermore, the cost of education at private institutions in country or for international students out of country is well beyond the means of most families anywhere in the world. For students in countries where higher education is for the elite, or is perhaps in transition from elite to mass, the most important role of women's colleges and universities may be in providing access at all, regardless of the gender composition of the institution.

Where higher education is available at the mass or universal level nationally, women's colleges and universities may still be selective in their admission, but they may need to dip further into the applicant pool and provide more financial incentives than coeducational schools of similar reputation. So the women's colleges in Australia, Canada, Italy, Japan, South Korea, and the United Kingdom had to "sell" themselves a bit more. Though I am cautious in using the neoliberal concept of the market to discuss the ecosystem of higher education, the reality is that talented students have options, and single-sex education is decreasing in popularity in many places. Women's colleges must compete with coeducational peers to attract students. With limited resources, they must also be sensitive to investing scholarship dollars wisely and leveraging admission of nonscholarship students. Coeducational institutions face the same financial challenges, but they have the advantage of having up to twice as many potential applicants (men *and* women) and greater appeal to many young women looking at their options for higher education. Overall, the national picture for higher education access and affordability shapes the role and operation of women's colleges and universities within countries, just as the presence of women's institutions shapes the internal landscape of opportunities for students.

Turning to the "local" element of the glonacal heuristic, the influence of local culture on the students attending the institutions in this study and what happened there was clear. Japanese institutions promoted both excellence in nontraditional STEM fields and tacit adherence to the "good wife, wise mother" (*ryōsai kenbo*) philosophy of women's education. Some upper-class white youth in Australia, Italy, and the United Kingdom saw the residential women's colleges as a way to make connections with daughters of similar families. Kenyan faculty and administrators worried about the safety and vigor of the "girl children" under their supervision, away from home. Indian institutions negotiated the intricate religious, tribal, caste, ethnic, class, and linguistic diversity inherent in contemporary Indian society.

As advised by Marginson and Rhoades (2002), Morley (2010), Shahjahan and Kezar (2013), Stromquist (1990, 2005), and Vavrus (2002), I considered the local context as often as possible when presenting the five main roles of women's colleges and universities in the countries I visited, but I attempted to connect it to the national and global contexts in which the local is embedded and with which it interacts. In doing so, I hoped to illustrate the dynamic nature of the social, cultural, and political ecology in which women's colleges and universities attempt to create change and are called upon to react to change.

Gender, Social Class, and Culture

Just as women's colleges and universities in the twenty-first century intersect with global, national, and local contexts, they also operate at the intersection of gender with other factors that will, in part, determine their futures. In particular, social class and culture intersected with gender to influence individual students, faculty, and leaders, as well as policy and program decisions made within the institutions. These intersections may also largely determine the future of women's colleges and universities locally, nationally, and globally.

Research has shown that social class is an even larger determinant of girls' educational opportunities than gender (Kabeer, 2005; Morley, 2010; Morley & Lugg, 2009). Regardless of gender, poor children around the world are less likely than wealthier children of their age to attend and persist in school (International Bank for Reconstruction and Development and the World Bank, 2011; Jensen, 2011; Kabeer, 2005; UNESCO, n.d.). Studies have shown that poor families have educational aspirations for their daughters that are as high, or nearly so, as for their sons, even if in reality those families cannot or do not make opportunities equally available (Stromquist, 2001b). For girls from poor families who have obtained elementary and secondary education, social class remains a key factor in their access to higher education (Morley & Lugg, 2009; Stromquist, 2001b). While visiting the women's colleges and universities in this study, I heard administrators' concerns about access and affordability for students from diverse social class backgrounds. This concern is not unique to women's institutions, but it was clearly evident at several institutions I studied.

Because of their individual histories, the women's colleges and universities in this study are positioned differently in relation to serving students from poorer families. MEWC has financial backing from a relatively wealthy government and, while only a few decades old, it can rely on government funding to provide free tuition to all students and computer scholarships for those students who need them. KIST is also a young institution, privately backed by a wealthy Kenyan founder. He and his institutional leadership must decide how much of his money to invest in growing the university, and whether the money is best spent on facilities and staffing or on scholarships for capable but financially needy students who otherwise would have to rely on government and private loans. For the first few years, the founder told me, he was able to make scholarships available to all students who needed them, but after the financial crisis set in it was no longer possible, and several students had to leave school midyear. The revolutionary roots of WFU have some modern limitations; since China's Ministry of Education upgraded it to general university status in 2002, students must pay tuition or cover their expenses with government scholarships or private loans. Longer-established institutions in Australia, Canada, India, Italy, Japan, South Korea, and the United Kingdom had endowments and other sources of private funding to provide scholarship aid to some students in need.

Other than at MEWC, no institutional leaders believed that they had the financial resources to support as many poor students as they wished they could. They acknowledged that there were women who would not be able to attend their institutions because of the cost, even with public or private loans. What other options did these women have? According to one rector, they might seek a government institution in their hometown, or pursue vocational training. But a university education was most likely out of reach. There are millions of men worldwide in the same position, of course, but as noted in chapters 1 and 3, men without a postsecondary credential have more options—and can earn more money—than women with the same level of education.

The ability of women's colleges and universities to continue to support women from less wealthy backgrounds (even if not at the levels they would like) was linked in almost every case (except KIST) to trends in public funding for higher education.[1] Because they are linked to government university tuition set-

1. A full analysis of public funding, social class, and access to higher education is beyond the scope of this book. Public and private investment in higher education is a changing landscape in most of the world, with some nations investing more public funds, some investing less, and many

ting, scholarship schemes, and student subsidies, they cannot fully control the cost to a student of her education. Thus there are limitations on how much institutions can do to overcome the constraints of social class on women's ability to participate in higher education. These limitations extend to coeducational institutions, but at women's colleges and universities, any and all poor students whom they are able to support will be women. At the institutional level, gender is not part of the equation of funding students.

Although analyses of social class, gender, and higher education often focus on opportunities for poor women, the majority of students at the women's colleges and universities I studied were from middle-class and wealthy families. Gender empowerment and economic development are not necessarily priorities for these students. As Jayaweera (1997b) noted, higher education "tends to be valued in non-poor families as a personal attainment rather than as an agent of economic empowerment for women" (p. 252). Students and families viewed the highly selective women's colleges and universities in my study as opportunities not only to earn an educational credential but also to burnish—or lay claim to—membership in elite social circles. The historic role of some of these institutions in educating members of the upper social classes carried over in their reputations, no matter the current socioeconomic composition of the student body. Some students reported that, to them, attending an elite women's institution was more advantageous in terms of signaling a particular social class than attending a coeducational institution.

Just as social class interacts with gender in societal and higher education milieux, culture plays a substantial role in the status, role, and future of the women's colleges and universities in this book. Without question, culture—and religion in particular—influences individual, family, and community values about girls' and women's education (Knight, 2004; Naidoo & Moussly, 2009). This influence came through across institutions I studied, in relation to the specifics of local culture. In some regions (e.g., Australia, East Asia, Europe, North America), majority cultures support and even prefer coeducational higher education. Waning interest in women's colleges is a threat to their continued existence, as is clearly seen in the United States and the United Kingdom. A relative handful of US women's colleges have survived, many of which will have to consider closing, merging, radically changing their academic programs, or admitting men in order to stay viable as small, private institutions (Biemiller, 2011;

---

changing their patterns of funding to leverage increased access. Readers interested in understanding the evolving state of higher education funding worldwide might begin with Bruce Johnstone and Pamela Marcucci's (2010) excellent book *Higher Education Worldwide: Who pays? Who should pay?*

Miller-Bernal, 2011). Only one women's institution remains in Canada, and a few dozen remain across Europe. The larger culture is one in which young women prefer to apply to coeducational colleges and universities. There is no evidence that this trend is reversing.

From the perspective of attempting to introduce (not preserve) a single-sex sector in Kenyan higher education, cultural forces are also at work against the survival of a women's university. Although there are families who would not send their daughters to study at a coeducational university, the overall culture of mixed-gender higher education sets KIST apart in ways that may make it difficult to recruit students. KIST is a private university in a culture in which public universities are strongly preferred for reasons of both affordability and perceived quality. Unless the Kenyan government follows through with the idea of opening a women's university, it seems unlikely that a single-sex sector can get off the ground within a culture of coeducation and public higher education. For now, in a culture that favors educating sons over daughters, KIST faces an uphill climb in convincing families to pay private university costs. Unfortunately for KIST, the families most likely to prefer single-sex education for cultural reasons— those in the more rural, culturally conservative areas—are the least likely to be able to afford a private university.

In the Middle East and India, on the other hand, cultural values strongly support maintaining a women's higher education sector for the foreseeable future. While some students in India saw these cultural values as constraining their choices, they also reported positive experiences at the women's colleges and universities they attended. The strong cultural mandate for gender-segregated education in the UAE resulted in the establishment of parallel government-sponsored women's and men's colleges in each of the emirates, as well as a state-of-the-art women's liberal arts university with campuses in Abu Dhabi and Dubai (the university now also admits men and runs parallel, gender-segregated programs; see Lipka, 2012). The modern, gleaming campuses of the women's college and the university are testaments to the idea that separate does not mean inferior, and the policy of not charging Emirati nationals to attend means that women from diverse social-class backgrounds have full access to higher education. Even as the UAE took small steps toward mixed-gender education, no one I met at MEWC was in a particular hurry to eliminate opportunities for women to learn in spaces of their own. Students, faculty, and leaders were fierce defenders of maintaining the college for women only in order to keep it accessible to students from even the most conservative families.

The Indian case is perhaps the most interesting one when it comes to intersections of culture and gender in women's higher education. The overall system of Indian higher education contains private and government-sponsored men's, women's, and coeducational institutions. Though many students express a preference for coeducation, it is not as strong as in North America or Europe. And, in a context in which millions of potential students would be willing to attend *any* institution rather than none, personal preference for coeducation becomes less of a priority than the desire to get a higher education regardless of the gender composition of the student body.

Indian women's higher education institutions are not "the norm" in the sense of being the majority of colleges and universities open to women, but they are "normal" in the sense of being numerous, visible, and unremarkable (if not always a young woman's first choice). Currently, the culture for education in India not only favors continuing support (from students, families, government, and the public) for women's colleges and universities, but also expanding the sector to create more opportunities for women. It is not clear what will happen to support for single-sex colleges and universities if and when India reaches a point of mass to universal access to higher education. Will conservative religious and family values favor keeping over 2,500 women's institutions open? Will societal norms shift in a direction that more strongly supports coeducation? And will competition among institutions emerge, as it has in the United States, to affect differently positioned women's institutions in distinct ways? Will the elite institutions be able to remain all women, based on their histories, traditions, and financial backing, while less elite institutions will consider admitting men or merging into men's or coeducational institutions in order to attract students and remain viable? Leaders of the Indian colleges and university in my study diverged on the exact path of women's institutions in the future but converged around the idea that subsector differentiation was likely to occur. This differentiation—and thus differing outcomes across the women's education sector—would not come for decades yet, as the multiple, diverse cultures that make up the national environment for education are proceeding at varying paces on their ideas about gender equality. Preparing their institutions to best serve women—alone or with men—was a priority for all.

Social class and culture intersect with gender and ideas about women's roles in society in ways that influenced and will continue to influence women's colleges and universities around the world. Except in the (fortunately rare) circumstances in which cultural extremists violently enforce their opposition, history has resolved in the affirmative the question of whether girls and women should be educated. Social class, religion, and culture still play substantial roles in which girls and women in the world get an education, and they interact with local, national, and global forces to shape—and be shaped by—women's colleges and universities in the early twenty-first century.

A Means to an End or a Permanent Presence?

After considering five roles that women's colleges and universities play in different regions in the twenty-first century, I come to a final question: *Are women's colleges and universities a means to the end goal of gender equity, or will they be a permanent, distinctive sector in postsecondary education?* If one's definition of "gender equity" is limited to equal access to postsecondary education, then they are likely an important but impermanent feature of higher education worldwide. It will be time to celebrate when all girls and women, wherever they are born and into whatever circumstances, have access to education at the same rate as boys and men—with even more to celebrate when all children and adults, everywhere, have access to quality education. But once the access problem is solved, will there still be a role for women's colleges and universities? I argue that there is and will continue to be.

Access cannot be taken for granted and is the sine qua non of women's education. But equal access to higher education does not guarantee gender equality—it never has and likely never will. In her analysis of higher education and feminism in the Arab Gulf region, Findlow (2013) concluded, "high [postsecondary] participation levels themselves are insufficient grounds to claim that Gulf women are being freed via higher education from traditional hegemonic constraints" (p. 115). In a similar vein, Jayaweera (1997b) described gender inequality in Asia: "Despite the increasing access of women to higher education, it appears that the ideology of gender subordination embedded in Asian traditional social norms and transplanted Western colonial norms still restricts the autonomy of women in important issues that impinge on their quality of life" (p. 259). Access—via single-sex or coeducational higher education—is not enough.

The roles of women's colleges and universities in cultivating leaders, educating women in nontraditional fields, promoting gender empowerment, and acting as symbols of women's potential offer some possibilities for considering a viable future for these institutions even after equal access is achieved and sustained. Outside of women's studies programs and women's centers, coeducational institutions have made few attempts to be pacesetters for promoting gender equality. Many former men's colleges are not so much truly "coeducational" as they are men's colleges with some female students; women face chilly campus climates and remain the minority of faculty and institutional leaders, even where female students may now outnumber males (see, e.g., Miller-Bernal & Poulson, 2004, for a discussion of women's experiences at former men's colleges in the United States; Batson, 2008, on women at Oxford; Najar, 2013, on gender discrimination in Indian higher education; and Morley, 2006a, 2012, on access and equity in Nigeria, South Africa, Sri Lanka, Tanzania, and Uganda). Even where coeducational institutions may be attempting to counter gender discrimination on campus and in society, promoting transformation in the direction of gender equality is not high among institutional priorities. And, as many scholars of gender, development, and education have pointed out, access alone is not enough if the transformation of gender in society does not also occur (Ali, 2002; Brennan, King, & Lebeau, 2004; Findlow, 2013; Herz & Sperling, 2004; Hyer et al., 2008; Jayaweera, 1997a, 1997b; Kabeer, 2005; Malik & Courtney, 2011; Metcalfe, 2011; Nussbaum, 2004; Robinson-Pant, 2004; Stromquist, 1990, 1995, 2001b, 2002, 2012; Syed, 2010).

Women's colleges and universities surely play a role in access to higher education, and through the other roles they play they may also contribute to transforming gender construction and constraints in local, national, and global contexts. They are a means for individual and collective empowerment of women. Not all alumnae of these institutions will take up the call to public leadership for gender equity, but in their own lives, families, careers, and communities they will have the opportunities afforded them by their education. It is up to women and men who graduate from coeducational universities to do their part as well, for it will take more than women's college and university alumnae to make the changes necessary to create a gender-equitable society that is just, humane, and sustainable.

Multisite Case Study Research Design

In chapter 2, I provided a general description of my approach to this study, leaving to this appendix some of the more technical details of research perspective and design for those readers interested in aspects of methodology. I have previously reported on the methodology of this study (Renn, 2012)* and provide a synthesis and elaboration here.

Research Approach

In designing and conducting the study, I drew from feminist standpoint, postmodern feminist, and international/comparative educational research perspectives in the qualitative tradition. Qualitative research is ideal for studies such as this one that aim to understand a phenomenon (in this case, the roles women's colleges and universities) from the perspectives of institutional actors (students, faculty, executive leaders, alumnae) and surrounding artifacts (websites, institutional documents, education ministry policies; see Denzin & Lincoln, 2011). Qualitative studies rely on the researcher as "bricoleur" to interpret information gleaned through multiple methods and practices to create a "sequence of representations connecting the parts to the whole" (Denzin & Lincoln, 2011, p. 6).

A feminist standpoint perspective holds women at the center of the study (Harding, 1987, 2008; Harding & Norberg, 2005; Lather, 1992; Olesen, 2011), which is an appropriate standpoint for studying colleges and universities dedicated to educating women. A transnational feminist perspective proved to be particularly useful, as it "analyzes national and cross-national feminist organizing and action" and "examines bases of feminist mobilization, for example, class, race, ethnicity, religion, and regional struggles" (Olesen, 2011, p. 130). The tenets of transnational feminism include avoiding imposition of a Westernized view of feminism onto other contexts (Mendez & Wolf, 2011; Mendoza, 2002), which was important to me as I designed and conducted the study. Including aspects of postmodern feminism (see Harding, 1987; Olesen, 2011; Stromquist, 2000) was also important in considering that the

---

*Some sections of this appendix are drawn directly from that article and are used with permission.

diversity, commonalities, and contradictions that I observed around the world could not be compressed into a story of some imagined "universal womanhood" or "universal women's institution."

These perspectives influenced my research design and decisions. For example, I focus exclusively on institutions that educate women, illuminating gender as a central organizing power in societies around the world. The decision not to include a comparison group of coeducational institutions is consistent with feminist standpoint methodology (Harding, 1987; Olesen, 2011). From the start, I decided not to compare women at women's colleges and universities with those at coeducational ones, though that would also have been an interesting study. When it came to data interpretation and analysis, I was cautious (though some readers may point out where I could be more so) to avoid universalizing to some imagined "'generic' woman" (Stromquist, 2000, p. 421). It was important to maintain gender in local, national, and global contexts without essentializing women's experiences globally (Mendez & Wolf, 2011).

Consistent with tenets of feminist standpoint, transnational feminist, and postmodern perspectives, my international comparative research lens allowed for understanding women and women's institutions in social contexts. Instead of a series of atomized, single-country studies of women's higher education or a monolithic, smoothed-out aggregation of all data into singular conclusions, I sought commonalities and differences across national borders. Shahjahan and Kezar (2013) argued against what they term "methodological nationalism" and advocated a more global view of higher education systems of knowledge and power. I agree substantially with their caution against reinscribing global systems of power through research located in national containers, but for the purposes of understanding how women's colleges and universities contribute to higher education and society, it is necessary to consider national contexts of policy and practice. The different ways that national governments fund higher education for citizens affect decisions at the institutional level, for example, as do immigration policies. Although finance and immigration contribute to the global context of higher education beyond national borders, nation-states (which must be considered in the context of any individual institution) largely control them.

Stromquist (2005) called on researchers to conduct more international comparative studies of gender and education, and I designed my study to contribute to comparative literature on women in tertiary education. Vavrus and Bartlett (2006) recommended conducting comparative research through a vertical case study approach. Vertical case studies are consistent with feminist and postmodern perspectives on situating specific experiences within larger systems of power. In order to understand the cases from "contextual understanding and detailed micro-level research" (Vavrus & Bartlett, 2006, p. 96), I undertook a comparative, multisite vertical case study design. I used two primary strategies for data collection: (1) obtaining documents and records on national higher education systems and individual institutions; and (2) interviewing campus leaders, faculty, students, and, when possible, staff from ministries of education.

Research Site Selection

I followed principles of purposeful and maximum variation sampling in qualitative research (Miles, Huberman, & Saldaña, 2013) and Vavrus and Bartlett's (2006) recommendations regarding international comparative studies to select sites that vary by geography, culture, and institutional characteristics (e.g., size, curriculum, years of operation, and governance). I relied on Purcell, Helms, and Rumbley's (2005) compilation of information about international women's universities and colleges and a pilot study I conducted through the Women's Education Worldwide organization as a starting point for understanding the diversity and overall distribution of institutions worldwide. WEW is a loose association of leaders of women's colleges and universities from around the world. Founded at Mount Holyoke and Smith Colleges in the United States, the group has met biannually since 2004 (see www.womenseducation worldwide.org).

I decided to focus on four main criteria in selecting institutions: (1) supranational region (e.g., Indian subcontinent, sub-Saharan Africa, Western Europe); (2) institutional history and mission (e.g., liberal arts, STEM, adult education); (3) institutional control and governance (i.e., its relationship to the state, such as government sponsored, fully private, state related, or affiliation with a religious organization such as the Catholic Church); and (4) institutional type (e.g., free-standing women's institution, women's college affiliated with a women's or coeducational university, women's residential college within a coeducational university). I focused on these criteria because, based on the literature on gender, education, and development, they seemed likely to influence the roles that the institutions played. I excluded from consideration institutions that were less than 5 years old (e.g., Asian University for Women, African Rural University) on the basis that they would not yet be likely to have established their roles in the higher education system. I also excluded from the study some women's institutions in regions of the world where there existed civil unrest, war, or other threats to safety during the time of my data collection.

I purposefully selected thirteen institutions in ten nations (Australia, Canada, China, India, Italy, Japan, Kenya, South Korea, the UAE, and the United Kingdom) for the ways they represent types and statuses of women's colleges and universities globally. I used contacts in the WEW network to identify six institutions and to facilitate access to campuses; in cases that lacked WEW connections, I initiated communication with the rector, principal, or president, locating their names and email addresses through institutional webpages and online searches, including ministries of education, conference proceedings, and publication records. When searching for information for institutions for which English was not the primary language, or that lacked an English translation of the webpage and used a language I do not read with adequate skill, I enlisted the help of speakers of the relevant languages (Arabic, Chinese, and Japanese) to locate information online. I explained my study to institutional leaders and asked to meet with them when I would be in country (sometimes my date was set in advance, other times I negotiated best dates with the institution). I asked for the name of a dean or faculty member who could help me set up additional meetings with faculty, leadership, and students during my visit. This dean or faculty member and I typically discussed schedules and opportunities to maximize my time at the campus, and my itineraries were filled from early to quite late in the day (or evening).

While in India, Japan, South Korea, the UAE, and the United Kingdom, I also toured a number of other women's campuses not included in the study and met informally with their institutional leaders to learn more about the context for women's colleges and universities in those countries. And, as noted in chapter 2, in spite of my and others' best efforts in advance of and during the data collection phases, I was unable to identify women's colleges or universities operating in Central or South America to include in the study. Since completing data collection, I have located a website for a women's university in Lima, Peru, and I welcome suggestions from readers for other institutions to include in future studies.

Data Collection and Analysis

I conducted site visits from February 2009 through June 2011. In keeping with Vavrus and Bartlett's (2006) recommendations regarding vertical case study, I aimed to collect data from all levels of the institution and from formal and informal sources. Data for each site include documents and websites, interviews, student focus groups, and on-site observations. I spent a week at each campus conducting formal interviews and focus groups. Depending on available opportunities for informal observations of campus life, I attended events (e.g., concerts, lectures, book launches) open to the public, read campus publications, sat in cafeterias and libraries, and joined students and faculty for meals, recreation, and cultural activities. Formal interviews at each institution included senior leadership (typically the president, rector, or provost level), faculty leaders (department chairs, research center directors), and other faculty (across departments). I most often met with students in focus groups composed of students identified for me by faculty or staff from one or more classes or student clubs. In six countries I also conducted interviews with ministry of education officials. In China, a faculty member familiar with Chinese higher education and with women's issues translated during two administrator interviews and one student focus group. All other interviews and focus groups were in English, sometimes with informal translation by participants to clarify points for one another and for me. The Michigan State University Institutional Review Board and the research committees of institutions for which local permission was required approved the study.

As noted in chapter 2, data amounted to 198 hours of recorded individual interviews, forty-eight hours of focus groups, and three and a half linear feet of campus artifacts. I created a profile of each institution compiled from online documents, plus a personal database of information gleaned from online and documentary sources about each nation. Since my visits, I have kept up with campus news reports, relevant local media, and government documents, though the data I report in this book come from the time I was in the field.

In keeping with the tradition of open coding in qualitative research (Coffey &

Atkinson, 1996; Miles, Huberman, & Saldaña, 2013), data analysis followed an inductive approach to code and theme development. I employed both open coding procedures and a priori codes (Boyatzis, 1998) developed from a pilot study I conducted with WEW institutional leaders and a study conducted at a WEW student leaders conference in 2008 (reported in Renn & Lytle, 2010). I collected and analyzed data over three academic years, which allowed me to engage in an iterative process of interpretation by checking new themes as they emerged in later cases against data collected in earlier cases.

Researcher Positionality

The positionality or subjectivity of the researcher is a key factor in qualitative research generally (Marshall & Rossman, 2010) and feminist research in particular (Lather, 1992). Franks (2002) defined positionality within "cross-ideological feminist social research" as "a cultural concept relating to gender, ethnicity, culture and so on" (p. 43). Accordingly, it is important to know that I am a US-based professor of higher education, which means that I study higher education and teach about it to graduate students who are interested in working as postsecondary administrators, faculty members, or policymakers. I am also a former university student affairs administrator. My graduate education and professional lives have occurred in public and private coeducational colleges and universities, including working for one year in student affairs at formerly all-women Wheaton College (United States), the year that their first male students matriculated. I am white, able-bodied, and in my mid-40s; people who met me or saw me around campus likely correctly ascertained these characteristics and may have ascribed these identities to me.

I got my bachelor's degree from one of the oldest women's colleges in the world, Mount Holyoke College (United States), which remains a small, private liberal arts college for just over two thousand women. My affiliation with Mount Holyoke facilitated my access to the WEW organization and provided a level of "insider" status at the institutions I visited. I am loyal to my alma mater and proud of its ongoing contributions to educating women from around the world, though I recognize that coeducational colleges and universities in the United States and internationally educate a far greater number of women. I am committed to increasing gender equity and women's access to higher education worldwide, and began the study with an open mind on the question of whether coeducational or single-sex institutions best achieved these goals. Over the course of the study, I developed affection for the institutions I visited and for their students, faculty, and leaders. But I remain open to the idea that women's colleges and universities may not be the best or only way to achieve gender equity and access to higher education.

Trustworthiness

I use the concept of trustworthiness drawn from the qualitative research paradigm, rather than validity, which is more often used in reference to quantitative and statistical research (Marshall & Rossman, 2010). I attempted to bolster trustworthiness in data collection, analysis, and interpretation. For example, I knew that as an outsider accessing participants through high-level officials I was likely to be pointed in the direction of individuals who might hold similar views about the institution, telling me what they thought those high-level officials wanted me to hear. When setting up appointments and conducting interviews, I asked if there were individuals who might feel differently and if I could speak to them as well. During interviews and focus groups, I also emphasized that my purpose was not to evaluate specific institutions and that I would use pseudonyms for institutions and people. Also, in consultation with scholars native to the countries I visited (but not involved in the study), I developed interview and focus group protocols using language and higher education concepts appropriate to local contexts. Terms for institutional leaders (principal, rector, president, chancellor) vary, for example, as do terms for a student's curriculum (course, syllabus, major, faculty, subject).

In analyzing data, I enhanced trustworthiness through consulting with native scholars as I developed codes and themes, checking developing interpretations against alternates, and seeking discrepant cases in the data (Boyatzis, 1998; Marshall & Rossman, 2010). I remained in email contact with several individuals whom I had interviewed and checked both facts—"Do I have this right about the way that funding/curriculum/governance works?"—and analysis—"It seems like the data related to access/climate / student leadership lead to a finding of X." In many cases, my contacts confirmed my analysis, but sometimes they corrected me or elaborated on my findings. Periodic meetings with members of WEW and other international higher education leaders provided additional opportunities to discuss emerging themes and to reexamine my interpretations. Discussions with women's college and university leaders, faculty, and students—as well as comparative and international higher education scholars, some of whom were native to the countries in my study— further affirmed that my interpretations were reasonable.

Limitations

There are several limitations to bear in mind regarding this study. First, nuanced interpretation based on visits of only several days to any higher education institution is impossible. In any academic year there are routine cycles that shift the emphasis of activity (e.g., welcome or orientation, midstream in an academic term, final exams) and events—planned or unplanned—that raise awareness of particular issues (e.g., a visit by dignitaries, a student-run festival, celebration of a state/religious/cultural holiday, a student or campus crisis, an off-campus incident such as a well-publicized sexual assault at another college). What I would observe and hear at the same campus might differ across the semester or year depending on what was at the forefront of attention.

Second, cultural differences and intercultural communication challenges exacerbate the first limitation. In spite of my attempts to use language fitting each campus context, there were still times that I realized that my participants and I were talking about different concepts, requiring me to adjust my thinking or return to ask more questions to clarify my understanding of what had been said. Additionally, in some cultures the desire to please teachers, elders, and visitors is very strong, and I had to make extra efforts to get my interviewees (especially students and younger faculty members) to correct a misunderstanding on my part or to disagree with another member of a focus group. Presumably, there were occasions when I was unaware of the need to circle back or to encourage corrections or disagreements.

Third, participant selection for interviews and focus groups was a combination of purposeful (i.e., based on positions held at the institution) and convenience (e.g., which students were available at the designated focus group time). It is likely that different combinations of participants would have yielded different data. As I noted in the section above on trustworthiness, recruiting participants through senior institutional leaders was likely to lead to a sample biased in favor of giving a positive impression of the institution.

Fourth, in a few interviews and focus groups, reliance on a translator may have resulted in miscommunication of my questions or respondents' replies. The presence of a faculty member as a translator in one student focus group in China may have influenced students' replies as well. Although I explained the concepts of informed consent and confidentiality—and assured the students that the faculty member / translator had agreed to keep their comments confidential—I assume that that person's presence influenced their responses. To account for this effect, I have limited the use of data from that session to only the information that I could confirm through other data from that institution.

Ajbaili, M. (2011, May 15). Saudi Arabia opens largest women's college in the world. *Al Arabiya News*. Retrieved from http://english.alarabiya.net/articles/2011/05/15/149218 .html.

Al-Ahmadi, H. (2011). Challenges facing women leaders in Saudi Arabia. *Human Resource Development International, 14*(2), 149–66.

Ali, S. S. (2002). Women's rights, CEDAW and international human rights debates: Toward empowerment? In J. L. Parpart, S. M. Rai, & K. Staudt (Eds.), *Rethinking empowerment: Gender and development in a global/local world* (pp. 61–78). London: Routledge.

Aliya, S., Sherin, V. S., & Nagalakshmi. (2011). Indian women in science and technology. In V. N. Dass & T. A. Rani (Eds.), *Universities for women: Challenges and perspectives* (pp. 123–52). Delhi: Women Press.

Allan, E. J., & Madden, M. (2006). Chilly classrooms for female undergraduate students: A question of method? *Journal of Higher Education, 77*, 684–711.

Al Qasimi, L. B. K. (2007, March). *Millennium development goals: United Arab Emirates Report*. Second Report. Abu Dhabi: UAE Ministry of the Economy.

Altbach, P. G. (2004). Preface. In F. B. Purcell, R. M. Helms, & L. Rumbley (Eds.), *Women's universities and colleges: An international handbook* (pp. ix–x). Rotterdam: Sense.

Ash, L., & Boyd, A. W. (2012, August 17). Women's colleges struggle to keep identity and enrollment. *USA Today*. Retrieved from http://usatoday30.usatoday.com/news/education/story/2012-08-01/womens-colleges-enrollment/57103700/1.

Associated Press. (2009, September 30). Saudi king's university slammed for coed classes: report. Retrieved from www.guardian.co.uk/world/feedarticle/8733445.

Bailey, P. (2001). Active citizen or efficient housewife? The debate over women's education in early-twentieth-century China. In G. Peterson, R. Hayhoe, and Yongling Lu (Eds.), *Education, culture, and identity in twentieth-century China* (pp. 318–47). Ann Arbor: University of Michigan Press.

Bank, B. J., with Yelon, H. M. (2003). *Contradictions in women's education: Traditionalism, careerism, and community at a single-sex college*. New York: Teachers College Press.

Barone, C. (2011). Some things never change: Gender segregation in higher education across eight nations and three decades. *Sociology of Education, 84*(2), 157–76.

Batson, J. G. (2008). *Her Oxford*. Nashville, TN: Vanderbilt University Press.

Biemiller, L. (2011, September 11). Women's colleges try new strategies for success. *Chronicle of Higher Education.* Retrieved from http://chronicle.com/article/Womens-Colleges-Try-New/128935.

———. (2013, February 4). Armed with data, a women's college tries a transformation. *Chronicle of Higher Education.* Retrieved from http://chronicle.com/article/A-Womens-College-Tries-a/136969.

Bird, E. (2002). The academic arm of the women's liberation movement: Women's studies 1969–1999 in North America and the United Kingdom. *Women's Studies International Forum, 25*(1), 139–49.

Bourdieu, P., & Passeron, J.-C. (1990). *Reproduction in education, society, and culture* (2nd ed.). Thousand Oaks, CA: SAGE.

Boyatzis, R. E. (1998). *Transforming qualitative information: Thematic analysis and code development.* Thousand Oaks, CA: SAGE.

Bradley, K. (2000). The incorporation of women into higher education: Paradoxical outcomes? *Sociology of Education, 73*(1), 1–18.

Brennan, J., King, R., & Lebeau, Y. (2004). The role of universities in the transformation of societies: An international research project. Synthesis Report. London: Association of Commonwealth Universities.

Bron-Wojciechowska, A. (1995). Education and gender in Sweden: Is there any equality? *Women's Studies International Forum, 18*(1), 51–60.

Bruneau, M. F. (1992). Learned and literary women in late imperial China and early modern Europe. *Late Imperial China, 13*(1), 156–72.

Buchmann, C., & DiPrete, T. A. (2006). The growing female advantage in college completion: The role of parental resources and academic achievement. *American Sociological Review, 71,* 515–41.

Buchmann, C., DiPrete, T. A., & McDaniel, A. (2008). Gender inequalities in education. *Annual Review of Sociology, 34,* 319–37.

Buchmann, C., & Hannum, E. (2001). Education and stratification in developing countries: A review of theories and research. *Annual Review of Sociology, 27,* 77–102.

Burke, R. J., & Mattis, M. C. (2007). *Women and minorities in science, technology, engineering, and mathematics: Upping the numbers.* Cheltenham: Edward Elgar.

Butler, J. (1999). *Gender trouble: Feminism and the subversion of identity.* London: Routledge.

Caplan, P. J. (1994). *Lifting a ton of feathers: A woman's guide to surviving in the academic world.* Toronto: University of Toronto Press.

Capodilupo, C. M., Nadal, K. L., Corman, L., Hamit, S., Lyons, O. B., & Weinberg, A. (2010). The manifestation of gender microaggressions. In D. W. Sue (Ed.), *Microaggressions and marginality: Manifestation, dynamics, and impact* (pp. 193–216). San Francisco: John Wiley & Sons.

Carrigan, C., Quinn, K., & Riskin, E. A. (2011). The gendered division of labor among STEM faculty and the effects of critical mass. *Journal of Diversity in Higher Education, 4*(3), 131–46.

Chanana, K. (2007, February 17). Globalisation, higher education and gender: Changing subject choices of Indian women students. *Economic and Political Weekly 42,* 590–98.

Chandralaka, N. B. (2011). Women in information technology and law. In V. N. Dass & T. A. Rani (Eds.), *Universities for women: Challenges and perspectives* (pp. 263–71). Delhi: Women Press.

Chapman, C., Laird, J., Ifill, N., & KewalRamani, A. (2011). *Trends in high school dropout and completion rates in the United States: 1972–2009*. NCES 2012-006. Washington, DC: National Center for Education Statistics.

Charles, M., & Bradley, K. (2002). Equal but separate? A cross-national study of sex segregation in higher education. *American Sociological Review, 67*, 573–99.

———. (2009). Indulging our gendered selves? Sex segregation by field of study in 44 countries. *American Journal of Sociology, 114*, 924–76.

Charles, M., & Grusky, D. B. (2004). *Occupational ghettos: The worldwide segregation of women and men*. Stanford, CA: Stanford University Press.

Chege, F. N., & Sifuna, D. N. (2006). *Girls' and women's education in Kenya: Gender perspectives and trends*. Nairobi: UNESCO.

Church, R. L., & Sedlak, M. W. (1976). The antebellum college and academy. In R. L. Church & M. W. Sedlak (Eds.), *Education in the United States: An interpretive history* (pp. 23–51). New York: Free Press.

Coats, M. (1994). *Women's education*. Buckingham: Society for Research into Higher Education and Open University Press.

Coffey, A., & Atkinson, P. (1996). *Making sense of qualitative data: Complementary research strategies*. Thousand Oaks, CA: SAGE.

Colclough, C. (2008). Global gender goals and the construction of equality: Conceptual dilemmas and policy practice. In S. Fennell & M. Arnot (Eds.), *Equality in a global context: Conceptual frameworks and policy perspectives* (pp. 51–66). London: Routledge.

Collins, P. H. (2000). *Black feminist thought: Knowledge, consciousness, and the politics of empowerment*. New York: Routledge.

Constantinople, K. A., Cornelius, R., & Gray, J. (1988). The chilly climate: Fact or artifact? *Journal of Higher Education, 59*, 527–50.

Conway, J. K. (2001). *A woman's education*. New York: Alfred A. Knopf.

Council for the Advancement of Standards in Higher Education. (2012). *CAS professional standards for higher education* (8th ed.). Washington, DC: Council for the Advancement of Standards in Higher Education.

Crawford, M., & McLeod, M. (1990). Gender in the college classroom: An assessment of the "chilly climate" for women. *Sex Roles: A Journal of Research, 23*, 101–25.

Creighton, J. V. (2004, June 2). Address to the Women's Education Worldwide meeting. Retrieved from https://www.mtholyoke.edu/joannecreighton/pen_wewo4.

———. (2007, May 21). Why we need women's colleges. *Boston Globe*. Retrieved from www .boston.com/news/education/higher/articles/2007/05/21/why_we_need_womens_ colleges/.

Crenshaw, K. W. (1991). Mapping the margins: Intersectionality, identity politics, and violence against women of color. *Stanford Law Review, 43*, 1241–99.

Cress, C. M. (2002). Campus climate. In A. M. Martinez & K. A. Renn (Eds.), *Women in higher education: An encyclopedia* (pp. 390–97). Santa Barbara, CA: ABC-CLIO.

Cress, C. M., Astin, H. S., Zimmerman-Oster, K., & Burkhardt, J. C. (2001). Developmental outcomes of college students' involvement in leadership activities. *Journal of College Student Development, 42*, 15–27.

Daly, M. (2005). Gender mainstreaming in theory and practice. *Social Politics: International Studies in Gender, State & Society, 12*(3), 433–50.

Dan, H., & Zhu, Z. (2012, August 11). Women assume bigger role. *China Daily USA*.

Retrieved from http://usa.chinadaily.com.cn/epaper/2012–11/08/content_15894798 .htm.

DeBra, E. (1997). Women's colleges in the United States: A historical context. In I. Harwarth, M. Maline, & E. DeBra, *Women's colleges in the United States: History, issues, and challenges* (pp. 1–20). Washington, DC: National Institute on Postsecondary Education, Libraries, and Lifelong Learning, US Department of Education.

Denzin, N. K., & Lincoln, Y. S. (2011). Introduction. In N. K. Denzin & Y. S. Lincoln (Eds.), *The SAGE handbook of qualitative research* (4th ed.) (pp. 1–20). Thousand Oaks, CA: SAGE.

Dill, B. T., & Zambrana, R. E. (2009). Critical thinking about inequality: An emerging lens. In B. T. Dill & R. E. Zambrana (Eds.), *Emerging intersections: Race, class, and gender in theory, policy and practice* (pp. 1–21). New Brunswick, NJ: Rutgers University Press.

Donovan, C., Hodgson, B., Scanlon, E., & Whitelegg, E. (2005). Women in higher education: Issues and challenges for part-time scientists. *Women's Studies International Forum, 28,* 247–58.

EdStats. (2013). Education statistics. Washington, DC: World Bank. Retrieved from http://data.worldbank.org/data-catalog/ed-stats.

Feng, J. (2009). *The making of a family saga: Ginling College.* Albany: State University of New York Press.

Findlow, S. (2013). Higher education and feminism in the Arab Gulf. *British Journal of Sociology of Education, 34*(1), 112–31.

Fischer, K. (2008, May 2). Top colleges admit fewer low-income students: Pell Grant data show a drop since 2004. *Chronicle of Higher Education.* Retrieved from http://chronicle.com/weekly/v54/i34/34a00103.htm.

Fiske, E. B. (2012). *World atlas of gender equality in education.* Paris: UNESCO.

Franks, M. (2002). Feminisms and cross-ideological feminist social research: Standpoint, situatedness and positionality—Developing cross-ideological feminist research. *Journal of International Women's Studies, 3*(2), 38–50.

Ganguly-Scrase, R. (2000). Diversity and the status of women: The Indian experience. In L. Edwards & M. Roces (Eds.), *Women in Asia: Tradition, modernity and globalization* (pp. 86–111). Ann Arbor: University of Michigan Press.

Goby, V. P., & Erogul, M. S. (2011). Female entrepreneurship in the United Arab Emirates: Legislative encouragements and cultural constraints. *Women's Studies International Forum, 34*(4), 329–34.

Goldin, C., Katz, L. F., & Kuziemko, I. (2006). The homecoming of the American college women: The reversal of the college gender gap. NBER Working Paper 12139. Cambridge, MA: National Bureau of Economic Research. Retrieved from www.nber.org/papers/w12139.

Government of India. (2010–11). *Annual Report, 2010–11.* New Delhi: Ministry of Human Resources and Development.

Gunawardena, C., Rasanayagam, Y., Leitan, T., Bulumulle, K., & Abeyasekera-Van Dort, A. (2006). Quantitative and qualitative dimensions of gender equity in Sri Lankan Higher Education. *Women's Studies International Forum, 29*(6), 562–71.

Gwalani, P. (2013, March 22). Many women in higher education sector avoid top posts. *Times of India.* Retrieved from http://timesofindia.indiatimes.com/home/education/

news/Many-women-in-higher-education-sector-avoid-top-posts/articleshow/19119075 .cms.

Haddad, G., & Altbach, P. G. (2009). Introduction. In R. B. Ludeman, K. J. Osfield, E. I. Hidalgo, D. Oste, & H. W. Wang (Eds.), *Student affairs and services in higher education: Global foundations, issues and best practices* (pp. xiii–xiv). Paris: UNESCO.

Hall, R. M., & Sandler, B. R. (1982). *The campus climate: A chilly one for women?* Report of the Project on the Status and Education of Women. Washington, DC: Association of American Colleges.

———. (1984). *Out of the classroom: A chilly campus climate for women?* Report of the Project on the Status and Education of Women. Washington, DC: Association of American Colleges.

Harding, S. (Ed.). (1987). *Feminism & methodology.* Bloomington: Indiana University Press.

Harding, S. (2008). *Sciences from below: Feminisms, postcolonialities, and modernities.* Durham, NC: Duke University Press.

Harding, S., & Norberg, K. (2005). New feminist approaches to social science methodologies: An introduction. *Signs, 30,* 2009–19.

Hardwick-Day. (2008). *What matters in college after college: A comparative alumnae research study.* West Hartford, CT: Women's College Coalition. Retrieved from www.womens colleges.org/news/pdfs/WCC-What_Matters_March08.pdf.

Hart, J., & Fellabaum, J. (2008). Analyzing campus climate studies: Seeking to define and understand. *Journal of Diversity in Higher Education, 1*(4), 222–34.

Harwarth, I. B. (Ed.). (1997). *A closer look at women's colleges.* Washington, DC: US Department of Education Office of Educational Research and Improvement, National Institute on Postsecondary Education, Libraries, and Lifelong Learning.

Harwarth, I. B., & Fasanelli, F. (1997). Women's colleges in the United States, recent issues and challenges. In I. Harwarth, M. Maline, & E. DeBra, *Women's colleges in the United States: History, issues, and challenges* (pp. 21–42). Washington, DC: National Institute on Postsecondary Education, Libraries, and Lifelong Learning, US Department of Education.

Hasan, Z. (2008). A college of one's own. *India International Centre Quarterly, 34*(3/4), 208–21.

Healy, G., Özbilgin, M., & Aliefendiğlu, H. (2005). Academic employment and gender: A Turkish challenge to vertical sex segregation. *European Journal of Industrial Relations, 11*(2), 247–64.

Heller, J. R., Puff, C. R., & Mills, C. J. (1985). Assessment of the chilly college climate for women. *Journal of Higher Education, 56,* 446–60.

Herz, B., & Sperling, G. B. (2004). *What works in girls' education: Evidence and policies from the developing world.* New York: Council on Foreign Relations.

Horowitz, H. L. (1984). *Alma mater: Design and experience in the women's colleges from their nineteenth-century beginnings to the 1930s.* New York: Alfred A. Knopf.

———. (1994). *The power and passion of M. Carey Thomas.* New York: Alfred A. Knopf.

Hurtado, S., Griffin, K. A., Arellano, L., & Cuellar, M. (2008). Assessing the value of climate assessments: Progress and future directions. *Journal of Diversity in Higher Education, 1*(4), 204–21.

Hurtado, S., Milem, J. F., Clayton-Pedersen, A. R., & Allen, W. R. (1998). Enhancing campus climates for racial/ethnic diversity: Educational policy and practice. *Review of Higher Education, 21*(3), 279–302.

Hyer, K. E., Ballif-Spanvill, B., Peters, S. J., Solomon, Y., Thomas, H., & Ward, C. (2008). Gender inequalities in educational participation. In D. B. Holsinger & W. J. Jacob (Eds.), *Inequality in education: Comparative and international perspectives* (pp. 128–48). Hong Kong: Comparative Education Research Centre.

India Today. (2012a). India's best colleges. Arts: 2012 vs 2011. Retrieved from http://india today.intoday.in/bestcolleges/2012/comparecollege.jsp?stream=Arts&year1=2012& year2=2011.

———. (2012b). India's best colleges. Science: 2012 vs 2011. Retrieved from http://india today.intoday.in/bestcolleges/2012/comparecollege.jsp?stream=Science&year1=2012 &year2=2011.

Indiresan, J. (2002). *Education for women's empowerment: Gender-positive initiatives in pace-setting women's colleges*. Delhi: Konark.

———. (2011). Moving beyond academics: Gender positive initiatives in pace setting women's institutions in India. In V. N. Dass & T. A. Rani (Eds.), *Universities for women: Challenges and perspectives* (pp. 31–53). Delhi: Women Press.

International Bank for Reconstruction and Development and the World Bank. (2011). *World development report 2012: Gender equality and development*. Washington, DC: International Bank for Reconstruction and Development and the World Bank.

Ishii, N. K. (2004). *American women missionaries at Kobe College, 1873–1909: New dimensions in gender*. New York: Routledge.

Jamjoom, F. B., & Kelly, P. (2013). Higher education for women in the Kingdom of Saudi Arabia. In L. Smith & A. Abouammoh (Eds.), *Higher education in Saudi Arabia* (pp. 117–25). Dordrecht: Springer.

Jaschik, S. (2008, February 15). Converts to leading women's colleges. *Inside Higher Ed*. Retrieved from www.insidehighered.com/news/2008/02/15/women.

Jayaweera, S. (1997a). Women, education and empowerment in Asia. *Gender and Education, 9*(4), 411–24.

———. (1997b). Higher education and the economic and social empowerment of women—the Asian experience. *Compare: A Journal of Comparative and International Education, 27*(3), 245–61.

Jensen, L. (Ed.) (2011). *Millennium development goals 2011*. Second Report. New York: United Nations Development Program. Retrieved from www.undp.org.ae/Upload/ Doc/NMDGs_Eng2007_rec.pdf.

Johnstone, D. B., & Marcucci, P. N. (2010). *Higher education worldwide: Who pays? Who should pay?* Baltimore: Johns Hopkins University Press.

Kabeer, N. (2005). Gender equality and women's empowerment: A critical analysis of the third millennium development goal: 1. *Gender & Development, 13*(1), 13–24.

Karlekar, M. (1986). Kadambini and the Bhadralok: Early debates over women's education in Bengal. *Economic and Political Weekly, 21*(17), WS25–WS31.

Kaushik, S. K., Kaushik, S., & Kaushik, S. (2006). How higher education in rural India helps human rights and entrepreneurship. *Journal of Asian Economics, 17*, 29–34.

Kenya National Bureau of Statistics. (2011). Student enrollment 2005/06–2010/11. Retrieved from www.knbs.or.ke/university%20enrolment.php.

Keohane, N. O. (2003). Report of the steering committee for the women's initiative at Duke University. Durham, NC: Duke University. Retrieved from http://university-women.stanford.edu/reports/WomensInitiativeReport.pdf.

Kezar, A. J., & Moriarty, D. (2000). Expanding our understanding of student leadership development: A study exploring gender and ethnic identity. *Journal of College Student Development, 41*, 55–69.

Kim, M. M. (2001). Institutional effectiveness of women-only colleges: Cultivating students' desire to influence social conditions. *Journal of Higher Education, 72*(3), 287–321.

Kim, Y. K., & Sax, L. J. (2009). Student-faculty interactions in research universities: Differences by student gender, race, social class, and first-generation status. *Research in Higher Education, 50*, 437–59.

Kimmel, M. S. (2008). *Guyland: The perilous world where boys become men*. New York: Harper.

Kinzie, J., Thomas, A. D., Palmer, M. M., Umbach, P. D., & Kuh, G. D. (2007). Women students at coeducational and women's colleges: How do their experiences compare? *Journal of College Student Development, 48*(2), 145–65.

Klasen S. (2006). UNDP's gender-related measures: Some conceptual problems and possible solutions. *Journal of Human Development, 7*(2), 243–74.

Knight, L. W. (2004). Educating Asian women in women's colleges and universities: A world perspective. *Asian Journal of Women's Studies, 10*(4), 79–86.

Kodate, N., Kodate, K., & Kodate, T. (2010). Mission completed? Changing visibility of women's colleges in England and Japan and their roles in promoting gender equality in science. *Minerva, 48*, 309–30.

Kurshid, A. (2012). A transnational community of Pakistani Muslim women: Narratives of rights, honor, and wisdom in a women's education project. *Anthropology and Education Quarterly, 43*(3), 235–52.

Kwesiga, J. C., & Ssendiwala, E. N. (2006). Gender mainstreaming in the university context: Prospects and challenges at Makerere University, Uganda. *Women's Studies International Forum, 29*(6), 592–605.

Lal, M. (2009). Women's issues in India: An overview. *Intersections: Gender and sexuality in Asia and the Pacific, 22* [online]. Retrieved from http://intersections.anu.edu.au/issue22/lal.htm.

Lather, P. (1992). Critical frames in educational research: Feminist and post-structural perspectives. *Theory into Practice, 31*(2), 87–99.

Lee, M. (2011). A feminist political economic critique of the human development approach to new information and communication technologies. *International Communication Gazette, 73*(6), 524–38.

Leppel, K. (2002). Similarities and differences in the college persistence of men and women. *Review of Higher Education, 25*(4), 433–50.

Lewin, T. (2008, June 3). Sisters' colleges see a bounty in the Middle East. *New York Times*. Retrieved from www.nytimes.com/2008/06/03/education/03sisters.html.

Lihamba, A., Mwaipopo, R., & Shule, L. (2006). The challenges of affirmative action in Tanzanian higher education institutions: A case study of the University of Dar es Salaam, Tanzania. *Women's Studies International Forum, 29*(6), 581–91.

Lipka, S. (2012, March 11). Campuses engage students, U.S. style: Universities around the world adopt Western model of support services. *Chronicle of Higher Education.* Retrieved from http://chronicle.com/article/Universities-Around-the-World/131128/.

Louie, M. C. Y. (1995). *Minjung* feminism: Korean women's movement for gender and class liberation. *Women's Studies International Form, 18*(4), 417–30.

Ludeman, R. B., Osfield, K. J., Hidalgo, E. I., Oste, D., & Wang, H. S. (Eds.) (2009). *Student affairs and services in higher education: Global foundations, issues and best practices.* Paris: UNESCO.

Malik, S., & Courtney, K. (2011). Higher education and women's empowerment in Pakistan. *Gender and Education, 23*(1), 29–45.

Maranto, C., & Griffin, A. (2011). The antecedents of a "chilly climate" for women faculty in higher education. *Human Relations, 64*(2), 139–59.

Marginson, S., & Rhoades, G. (2002). Beyond national states, markets, and systems of higher education: A glonacal agency heuristic. *Higher Education, 43,* 281–309.

Marine, S. B. (2011). "Our college is changing": Women's college student affairs administrators and transgender students. *Journal of Homosexuality, 58*(9), 1165–86.

Marschke, R., Laursen, S., Nielsen, J. M., & Rankin, P. (2007). Demographic inertia revisited: An immodest proposal to achieve equitable gender representation among faculty in higher education. *Journal of Higher Education, 78*(1), 1–26.

Marshall, C., & Rossman, G. B. (2010). *Designing qualitative research* (5th ed.). Thousand Oaks, CA: SAGE.

McDaniel, A. (2010). Cross-national gender gaps in educational expectations: The influence of national-level gender ideology and educational systems. *Comparative Education Review, 54*(1), 27–50.

———. (2012). Women's advantage in higher education: Towards understanding a global phenomenon. *Sociology Compass 6/7,* 581–95.

McGuigan, D. G. (1970). *A dangerous experiment: 100 years of women at the University of Michigan.* Ann Arbor: University of Michigan Center for the Continuing Education of Women.

McMahon, W. W. (2009). *Higher learning, greater good: The private and social benefits of higher education.* Baltimore: Johns Hopkins University Press.

McVeigh, B. J. (1997). *Life in a Japanese women's college: Learning to be ladylike.* New York: Routledge.

Mendez, J. B., & Wolf, D. L. (2011). Feminizing global research / globalizing feminist research: Methods and practice under globalization. In S. N. Hesse-Biber (Ed.), *The handbook of feminist research: Theory and practice* (2nd ed.) (pp. 641–58). Thousand Oaks, CA: SAGE.

Mendoza, B. (2002). Transnational feminisms in question. *Feminist Theory, 3,* 295–314.

Metcalfe, B. D. (2011). Women, empowerment and development in Arab Gulf States: A critical appraisal of governance, culture and national human resource development (HRD) frameworks. *Human Resource Development International, 14*(2), 131–48.

Miles, M. B., Huberman, A. M., & Saldaña, J. (2013). *Qualitative data analysis: A methods sourcebook* (3rd ed.). Thousand Oaks, CA: SAGE.

Miller-Bernal, L. (2000). *Separate by degree: Women students' experiences in single-sex and coeducational colleges.* New York: Peter Lang.

———. (2004). Coeducation: An uneven progression. In L. Miller-Bernal & S. L. Poulson (Eds.), *Going coed: Women's experiences at formerly men's colleges and universities, 1950–2000* (pp. 3–21). Nashville, TN: Vanderbilt University Press.

———. (2006). Introduction. In L. Miller-Bernal & S. L. Poulson (Eds.), *Challenged by coeducation: Women's colleges since the 1960s* (pp. 1–20). Nashville, TN: Vanderbilt University Press.

———. (2011). The role of women's colleges in the twenty-first century. In L. M. Stulberg & S. L. Weinberg (Eds.), *Diversity in American higher education: Toward a more comprehensive approach* (pp. 221–31). New York: Routledge.

Miller-Bernal, L., & Poulson, S. L. (Eds.). (2004). *Going coed: Women's experiences at formerly men's colleges and universities, 1950–2000.* Nashville, TN: Vanderbilt University Press.

Ministry of Human Resource Development. (2006). Central Educational Institutions (Reservation in Admission) Act, 2006. New Delhi: Government of India. Retrieved from http://pib.nic.in/newsite/erelease.aspx?relid=23895.

Ministry of Women and Child Development. (2001). National policy for the empowerment of women. New Delhi: Government of India. Retrieved from http://wcd.nic.in/empwomen.htm.

Morley, L. (2006a). Hidden transcripts: The micropolitics of gender in Commonwealth universities. *Women's Studies International Forum, 29*(6), 543–51.

———. (2006b). Introduction: Including women: Gender in commonwealth higher education. *Women's Studies International Forum, 29,* 539–42.

———. (2010). Hyper-modernisation and archaism: Women in higher education internationally. In B. Riegraf, B. Aulenbacher, E. Kirsch-Auwärter, & U. Müller (Eds.), *Gender change in academia: Re-mapping the fields of work, knowledge, and politics from a gender perspective* (pp. 27–42). Wiesbaden: VS Verlag.

———. (2011). Sex, grades and power in higher education in Ghana and Tanzania. *Cambridge Journal of Education, 41*(1), 101–15.

———. (2012). Gender and access in Commonwealth higher education. *Advances in Education in Diverse Communities: Research, Policy and Praxis, 7,* 41–69.

Morley, L., & Lugg, R. (2009). Mapping meritocracy: Intersecting gender, poverty and higher educational opportunity structures. *Higher Education Policy, 22,* 27–60.

Morrison, Z., Bourke, M., & Kelley, C. (2005). "Stop making it such a big issue": Perceptions and experiences of gender inequality by undergraduates at a British University. *Women's Studies International Forum, 28*(2), 150–62.

Mount Holyoke College Office of Admissions. (2013). Hear from international students. Retrieved from https://www.mtholyoke.edu/admission/videos/hear_from_international_students.

Mukhopadhyay, C. C. (2004). How exportable are Western theories of gendered science? A cautionary word. In N. Kumar (Ed.), *Women and science in India: A reader* (pp. 137–78). New Delhi: Oxford University Press.

Nadeem, M., Mohsin, M. N., Ali, M. S., & Mohsin, M. S. (2012). Fair to dare sex: Empowering women for national development. *Interdisciplinary Journal of Contemporary Research in Business, 4*(4), 792–804.

Naidoo, A., & Moussly, R. (2009, February 28). Mixed reaction to co-education. *Gulf News.* Retrieved from http://gulfnews.com/news/gulf/uae/education/mixed-reaction-to-co-education-1.55433.

Najar, N. (2013, April 22). On India's campuses, female students speak out about "deep rooted" gender discrimination. *Chronicle of Higher Education* (p. A12). Retrieved from http://chronicle.com/article/Female-Scholars-Describe-Deep/138659/.

National Academies. (2008). *Gender faculty studies at research 1 institutions.* Washington, DC: National Research Council Committee on Women in Science and Engineering. Retrieved from http://sites.nationalacademies.org/PGA/cwsem/PGA_045079.

NCHERM. National Center for Higher Education Risk Management. (2012–13). Title IX Office for Civil Rights (OCR) case letter database. Retrieved from www.ncherm.org/resources/legal-resources/ocr-database/.

Nussbaum, M. C. (2004). Development cultures: New environments, new realities, new strategies. *Signs, 29*(2), 325–55.

Odejide, A., Akanji, B., & Odekunle, K. (2006). Does expansion mean inclusion in Nigerian higher education? *Women's Studies International Forum, 29*(6), 552–61.

OECD. Organisation for Economic Co-Operation and Development (2013). *Education at a glance 2013: OECD indicators.* Paris: OECD. http://dx.doi.org/10.1787/eag-2013-en.

Olesen, V. (2011). Feminist qualitative research in the millennium's first decade: Developments, challenges, prospects. In N. K. Denzin & Y. S. Lincoln (Eds.), *The SAGE handbook of qualitative research* (4th ed.) (pp. 129–46). Thousand Oaks, CA: SAGE.

Onsongo, J. K. (2011). *Promoting gender equity in selected public universities in Kenya.* Addis Ababa: Organisation for Social Science Research in Eastern and Southern Africa.

Osborne, R. L. (1995). The continuum of violence against women in Canadian universities: Toward a new understanding of the chilly campus climate. *Women's Studies International Forum, 18*, 5–6, 637–46.

Palmieri, P. A. (1987). From Republican motherhood to race suicide: Arguments on the higher education of women in the United States. In C. Lasser (Ed.), *Educating men and women together: Coeducation in a changing world* (pp. 49–66). Urbana-Champaign: University of Illinois Press.

———. (1995). *In Adamless Eden: The community of women faculty at Wellesley.* New Haven, CT: Yale University Press.

Pascarella, E. T., & Terenzini, P. T. (2005). *How college affects students: A third decade of research.* San Francisco: Jossey-Bass.

Perkin, H. (2006). History of universities. In J. J. F. Forest & P. G. Altbach (Eds.), *International handbook of higher education, part one: Global themes and contemporary challenges* (pp. 159–205). Dordrecht: Springer.

Peterson, M. W., & Spencer, M. G. (1990). Understanding academic culture and climate. In W. G. Tierney (Ed.), *Assessing academic climates and cultures*, vol. 68, *New directions for institutional research* (pp. 3–18). San Francisco: Jossey-Bass.

Phadke, S., Khan, S., & Ranade, S. (2011). *Why loiter? Women and risk on Mumbai streets.* New Delhi: Penguin.

Poulson, S. L., & Miller-Bernal, L (2004). Conclusion: Coeducation and gender equal education. In L. Miller-Bernal & S. L. Poulson (Eds.), *Going coed: Women's experiences in formerly men's colleges and universities, 1950–2000* (pp. 309–16). Nashville, TN: Vanderbilt University Press.

Purcell, F. B., Helms, R. M., & Rumbley, L. (Eds.) (2005). *Women's universities and colleges: An international handbook.* Rotterdam: Sense.

Qureshi, R., & Rarieya, J. F. A. (2007). *Gender and education in Pakistan.* Karachi: Oxford University Press.

Radha, N. N. (2011, October-December). A review on women's education in India. *Pragati,* 5(118), 32–50.

Raj, C. K. S. S. (2012). A new paradigm in management of higher educational institutes of government sector, India. *International Journal of Management, 3*(2), 32–42.

Renn, K. A. (2012). Roles of women's institutions in international contexts. *Higher Education, 64*(2), 177–91.

Renn, K. A., & Lytle, J. L. (2010). Women student leaders worldwide: Global perspectives on gender, leadership, and student involvement. *Journal of Student Affairs Research and Practice, 47*(2), 215–32.

Renn, K. A., & Reason, R. D. (2013). *College students in the United States: Characteristics, experiences, and outcomes.* San Francisco: Jossey-Bass.

Robinson-Pant, A. (2004). Education for women: Whose values count? *Gender and Education, 16*(4), 473–89.

Romano, R. C. (1996). A qualitative study of women student leaders. *Journal of College Student Development, 37,* 676–83.

Rose, B. (1992). *Tsuda Umeko and women's education in Japan.* New Haven, CT: Yale University Press.

Roudi-Fahimi, F., & Moghadam, V. M. (2003). Empowering women, developing society: Female education in the Middle East and North Africa. Policy Brief. Washington, DC: Population Reference Bureau. Retrieved from www.eldis.org/go/display&id=14732&type=Document#.UazAXOtyiEw.

Rowold, K. (2010). *The educated woman: Minds, bodies, and women's higher education in Britain, Germany, and Spain, 1865–1914.* New York: Routledge.

Rozario, S. (2001). Claiming the campus for female students in Bangladesh. *Women's Studies International Forum, 24*(2), 157–66.

Rupp, L. J. (1985). The women's community in the National Woman's Party, 1945 to the 1960s. *Signs, 10*(4), 715–40.

Sagaria, M. A. D. (1988). The case for empowering women as leaders in higher education. In M. A. D. Sagaria (Ed.), *Empowering women: Leadership development strategies on campus,* vol. 44, *New directions for student services* (pp. 5–12). San Francisco: Jossey-Bass.

Sahlin, C. L. (2005). Vital to the mission and key to survival: Women's studies at women's colleges. *National Women's Studies Association Journal, 17*(2), 164–70.

Sahni, R., & Shankar, V. K. (2012). Girls' higher education in India on the road to inclusiveness: On track but heading where? *Higher Education, 63,* 237–56.

Sandler, B. R. (1986). *The campus climate revisited: Chilly for women faculty, administrators, and graduate students.* Final Report. Washington, DC: Fund for the Improvement of Postsecondary Education.

Sax, L. J. (2001). Undergraduate science majors: Gender differences in who goes on to graduate school. *Review of Higher Education, 24*(2), 153–72.

Schofer, E., & Meyer, J. (2005). The world-wide expansion of higher education in the twentieth century. *American Sociological Review, 70,* 898–920.

Seat, K. K. (2008). *Providence has freed our hands: Women's missions the American encounter with Japan.* Syracuse, NY: Syracuse University Press.

Sen, A. (2004, June). What's the point of women's education? Remarks at Women's Education Worldwide 2004: Unfinished Agenda Conference, South Hadley, MA.

Shackleton, L., Riordan, S., & Simonis, D. (2006). Gender and the transformation agenda in South African higher education. *Women's Studies International Forum*, 29(6), 572–80.

Shahjahan, R. A., & Kezar, A. J. (2013). Beyond the "national container": Addressing methodological nationalism in higher education research. *Educational Researcher*, 42(1), 20–29.

Sharma, K. (2010, November 27). The other half: Unsafe for women? *The Hindu*. Retrieved from www.thehindu.com/opinion/columns/Kalpana_Sharma/article917408.ece.

Shizuko, K. (2012). Ryōsai kenbo: *The educational idea of the "good wife, wise mother" in modern Japan* (S. Filler, Trans.). Leiden, Netherlands: Brill Academic.

Singh, M. C. (2000). Gender, religion, and the "heathen lands": American missionary women in South Asia (1860s–1940s). New York: Garland.

Smith, D. G. (1990). Women's colleges and coed colleges: Is there a difference for women? *Journal of Higher Education*, 61, 181–95.

Smith, D. G., Wolf, L., & Morrison, D. (1995). Paths to success: Factors related to the impact of women's colleges. *Journal of Higher Education*, 66, 245–66.

Solomon, B. M. (1985). *In the company of education women*. New Haven, CT: Yale University Press.

Solorzano, D., Yosso, T., & Céja, M. (2000). Critical race theory, racial microaggressions, and campus racial climate: The experiences of African American college students. *Journal of Negro Education* 69(1/2), 60–73.

Somers, P., Cofer, J., Austin, J. L., Inman, D., Martin, T., Rook, S., et al. (1998). Faculty and staff: The weather radar of campus climate. In K. W. Bauer (Ed.), *Campus climate: Understanding the critical components of today's colleges and universities*, vol. 98, *New directions for institutional research* (pp. 35–52). San Francisco: Jossey-Bass.

Spender, D. (1987). *The education papers: Women's quest for equality in Britain, 1850–1912*. London: Routledge & Kegan Paul.

Sridhara, S. (2011). Women in agriculture, agricultural research and extension activities. In V. N. Dass & T. A. Rani (Eds.), *Universities for women: Challenges and perspectives* (pp. 153–92). Delhi: Women Press.

Stromquist, N. P. (1990). Gender inequality in education: Accounting for women's subordination. *British Journal of Sociology of Education*, 11(2), 137–53.

———. (1995). The theoretical and practical bases for empowerment. In C. Medel-Anonuevo (Ed.), *Women, education and empowerment: Pathways towards autonomy* (pp. 13–22). Hamburg: UNESCO Institute for Education.

———. (2000). Voice, harmony, and fugue in global feminism. *Gender and Education*, 12(4), 419–33.

———. (2001a). Gender studies: A global perspective of their evolution, contribution, and challenges to comparative higher education, *Higher Education*, 41(4), 373–87.

———. (2001b). What poverty does to girls' education: The intersections of class, gender and policy in Latin America. *Compare*, 31(1), 39–56.

———. (2002). Education as a means for empowering women. In J. L. Parpart, S. M. Rai, & K. Staudt (Eds.), *Rethinking empowerment: Gender and development in a global/local world* (pp. 22–38). London: Routledge.

———. (2005). Comparative and international education: A journal toward equality and equity. *Harvard Educational Review, 75*(1), 89–111.

———. (2012). The gender dimension in the World Bank's education strategy: Assertions in need of a theory. In S. J. Klees, J. Samoff, & N. P. Stromquist (Eds.), *The World Bank and education: Critiques and alternatives* (pp. 159–72). Rotterdam: Sense.

Sue, D. W. (2010). *Microaggressions in everyday life: Race, gender, and sexual orientation.* San Francisco: John Wiley & Sons.

Syed, J. (2010). Reconstructing gender empowerment, *Women's Studies International Forum, 33*(3), 283–94.

Teichler, U., Arimoto, A., & Cummings, W. K. (2013). *The changing academic profession: Major findings of a comparative survey.* Dordrecht: Springer.

Thelin, J. R. (2011). *A history of American higher education* (2nd ed.). Baltimore: Johns Hopkins University Press.

Thomas, A. D. (2008). Preserving and strengthening together: Collective strategies of U.S. women's college presidents. *History of Education Quarterly, 48*(4), 565–89.

Tidball, M. E. (1989). Women's colleges: Exceptional conditions, not exceptional talent, produce high achievers. In C. Pearson, D. L. Shavlik, & J. G. Touchton (Eds.), *Educating the majority: Women challenge tradition in higher education* (pp. 157–72). New York: Macmillan.

Tidball, M. E., Smith, D. G., Tidball, C. S., & Wolf-Wendel, L. E. (1999). *Taking women seriously: Lessons and legacies for educating the majority.* Phoenix: American Council on Education and Oryx Press.

Times of India. (2012, January 27). UGC mulls 20 exclusive univs, 800 colleges for women. Retrieved from http://articles.timesofindia.indiatimes.com/2012–01–27/news/30670061_1_new-colleges-model-colleges-scheme-autonomous-colleges.

Tjomsland, M. (2009). Women in higher education: A concern for development? *Gender, Technology and Development, 13*(3), 407–27.

Trow, M. (1974). Problems in the transition from elite to mass higher education. In *Policies for higher education.* From the General Report on the Conference for the Future Structures of Post-secondary Education (pp. 55–101). Paris: OECD.

———. (2010). *Twentieth-century higher education: Elite to mass to universal* (M. Burrage, Ed.). Baltimore: John Hopkins University Press.

UNDP. (1995). *Human development report.* New York: Oxford University Press.

———. (2013). MDG progress reports. New York: United Nations Development Programme. Retrieved from www.undp.org/content/undp/en/home/librarypage/mdg/mdg-reports/.

UNESCO. (n.d.). *Better life, better future.* Paris: United Nations. Retrieved from www.unesco.org/new/fileadmin/MULTIMEDIA/HQ/ED/pdf/BetterLife_ENG.pdf.

UNESCO Institute for Statistics. (2011a). Table 3b: Enrolment by ISCED level. Montreal: UNESCO Institute for Statistics. Retrieved from http://stats.uis.unesco.org/unesco/TableViewer/tableView.aspx?ReportId=175.

———. (2011b). Table 4d: Tertiary gross enrolment ratio. Montreal: UNESCO Institute for Statistics. Retrieved from http://stats.uis.unesco.org/unesco/TableViewer/tableView.aspx?ReportId=167.

———. (2011c). Table 5: Enrolment ratios by ISCED level. Montreal: UNESCO Institute for

Statistics. Retrieved http://stats.uis.unesco.org/unesco/TableViewer/tableView.aspx? ReportId=182.

———. (2011d). Table 8: School life expectancy (approximation method). Montreal: UNESCO Institute for Statistics. Retrieved from http://stats.uis.unesco.org/unesco/ TableViewer/tableView.aspx?ReportId=185.

———. (2011e). Table 14: Tertiary indicators. Montreal: UNESCO Institute for Statistics. Retrieved from http://stats.uis.unesco.org/unesco/TableViewer/tableView.aspx?Report Id=167.

United Nations. (2013). We can end poverty 2015: Millennium development goals. New York: United Nations. Retrieved from www.un.org/millenniumgoals/.

Unterhalter, E. (2005). Fragmented frameworks? Researching women, gender, education, and development. In S. Aikman & E. Unterhalter (Eds.), *Beyond access: Transforming policy and practice for gender equality in education* (pp. 15–35). Oxford: Oxfam GB.

Vavrus, F. (2002). Constructing consensus: The feminist modern and the reconstruction of gender. *Current Issues in Comparative Education, 5*(1), 51–63.

Vavrus, F., & Bartlett, L. (2006). Comparatively knowing: Making a case for the vertical case study. *Current Issues in Comparative Education, 8*(2), 95–103.

Vincent-Lancrin, S. (2008). The reversal of gender inequalities in higher education: An on-going trend. In S. Vincent-Lancrin (Ed.), *Higher education to 2030*, vol. 1, *Demography* (pp. 265–98). Paris: OECD Centre for Educational Research and Innovation.

Walby, S. (2005). Gender mainstreaming: Productive tensions in theory and practice. *Social Politics: International Studies in Gender, State & Society, 12*(3), 321–43.

Wall, S. (2008). Of heads and hearts: Women in doctoral education at a Canadian University. *Women's Studies International Forum, 31*(3), 219–28

Webber, M. (2005). "Don't be so feminist": Exploring student resistance to feminist approaches in a Canadian university. *Women's Studies International Forum, 28*(2), 181–94.

West, M. S., & Curtis, J. W. (2006). *AAUP faculty gender equity indicators 2006*. Washington, DC: American Association of University Professors.

Whitt, E. J. (1994). "I can be anything": Student leadership in three women's colleges. *Journal of College Student Development, 35*, 198–207.

Wolf-Wendel, L. E. (1998). Models of excellence: The baccalaureate origins of successful African American, European American, and Hispanic women. *Journal of Higher Education, 69*(2), 144–72.

———. (2000). Women-friendly campuses: What five institutions are doing right. *Review of Higher Education, 23*(3), 319–45.

———. (2002). Women's colleges. In A. M. Martinez Aleman & K. A. Renn (Eds.), *Women in higher education: An encyclopedia* (pp. 120–22). Santa Barbara, CA: ABC-CLIO.

Women's College Coalition. (n.d.). Women students at coeducational and women's colleges: How do their experiences compare? Decatur, GA: Women's College Coalition. Retrieved from www.womenscolleges.org/perspective/nsse-study.

Yang, S. (2008). *An analysis of women's development and gender equity at two universities in South China* (PhD dissertation, University of Minnesota). Available from ProQuest Dissertations and Theses Database (UMI No. 3313481).

Yuval-Davis, N. (2011). *The politics of belonging: Intersectional contestations.* Thousand Oaks, CA: SAGE.

Kristen A. Renn is a professor of higher, adult, and lifelong education at Michigan State University, where she is also the associate dean of undergraduate studies and director for student success initiatives. Her research focuses on college student learning and development, with an emphasis on diversity and equity in higher education. She studies women in higher education in US and global contexts and has published extensively on mixed-race college students and lesbian, gay, bisexual, and transgender students in the United States. She is an associate editor for international research and scholarship for the *Journal of College Student Development* and serves on editorial boards for the *American Educational Research Journal* and the *Journal of Diversity in Higher Education*. Prior to becoming a faculty member, she was a dean in the Office of Student Life at Brown University. She holds a bachelor's degree from Mount Holyoke College, a master's from Boston University, and a PhD from Boston College.